952
PL

D1598326

Raising a Baby the Government Way

Raising a Baby

The Douglass Series on Women's Lives
and the Meaning of Gender

the Government Way

Mothers' Letters
to the Children's Bureau,
1915–1932

Molly Ladd-Taylor

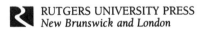 RUTGERS UNIVERSITY PRESS
New Brunswick and London

Library of Congress Cataloging-in-Publication Data

Raising a baby the government way.

(The Douglass series on women's lives and the
meaning of gender)
   Includes index.
   1. Child rearing—United States—History—Miscellanea.
2. Motherhood—United States—Miscellanea.   3. Pregnancy
—Miscellanea.   I. Ladd-Taylor, Molly, 1955–
II. United States. Children's Bureau.   III. Series.
HQ769.R168   1986   649'.1   85–31780
ISBN 0–8135–1177–1
British Cataloging-in-Publication
Information Available.

Contents

Acknowledgments

I am indebted to the staff of the National Archives for their assistance during my many visits there. My friend Ann Braude and my mother, Hylda Higginson Taylor, gave me encouragement and advice from the beginning of the project. I also wish to thank Nancy F. Cott, Paul Clifford, and George Chauncey, Jr. My sisters in the Wages for Housework Campaign, particularly Suzie Fleming and Selma James, first inspired me to seek the historical roots of our struggle to win recognition for women's work in the home. Without them, these letters would never have been published.

A Note
to the Reader

Throughout the editing, I have tried to preserve the authenticity and language of the letters. However, in order to ensure that punctuation errors and repetitions do not destroy the letters' effectiveness for the modern reader, I have occasionally deleted repetitious words or phrases, arranged the letters into paragraphs, and silently corrected punctuation where comprehensibility was at issue. Most spelling errors have been left as they originally appear in the letters. But I have added in brackets words or letters that were omitted and have corrected the spelling of words that were so misspelled as to be almost incomprehensible. Abbreviations and shortened forms of words have been left as they appear in the originals. Capitalization also follows the original documents. Finally, I have omitted the names of individuals (except public figures) and towns (except for large cities), so that the privacy of the correspondents is not in jeopardy.

This collection comprises the letters that I found to be especially evocative of women's lives. I have tried to select letters that reflect the breadth of women's work and shed light on their daily experiences and concerns. For this reason, I have included particularly revealing letters that were not originally addressed to the Children's Bureau but that found their way into the Children's Bureau correspondence. Because my limited resources and the unwieldy filing system of the Children's Bureau make a quantitative analysis of the letters' contents and the correspondents' background impossible—and because I believe that the real value of the letters lies in their human quality—I have not attempted to provide a representative sampling of the correspondence.

In order to give the reader a sense of the agency's attitude and approach, I have paraphrased portions of the Children's Bureau answers to some of the letters. Although most letters are attached to copies of the replies, unfortunately some of the answers are missing. Occasionally, I have omitted all or part of an existing response because it repeats information contained elsewhere in the chapter or because it is too detailed to be of interest to the general reader. For example, almost all the replies begin by listing the bulletins that were being sent the correspondent, sometimes referring her to certain pages in the bulletins. To avoid repetition, and to keep the focus of this book on the mothers themselves, I have omitted these parts of the Bureau responses. Throughout the book, I have tried to give the reader a sense of the agency's response to every issue raised in the correspondence. Although I have included the names of the Children's Bureau staff members who responded to the letters, I have generally omitted the names of physicians, public health officials, and social workers.

All the letters contained in this volume can be found among the Children's Bureau Records at the National Archives in Washington, D.C. The exact location and file number of each letter is given in the Appendix.

Raising a Baby the Government Way

Introduction:
Writing to the Children's Bureau

Before my father was born, my grandmother read *Infant Care* and *Prenatal Care*, the childrearing bulletins distributed by the Children's Bureau of the U.S. government. She found the pamphlets so helpful that she wrote the agency a letter. "They have been absolutely invaluable to me in preparing for and caring for my first baby," Alice Taylor Ladd told the government agency in 1917.[1] Although she died when I was a child, I stumbled upon my grandmother's letter years later at the National Archives. Researching motherhood and women's work in U.S. history, I had accidentally uncovered a bit of my own past. Finding my grandmother's letter inspired me to compile this collection of letters by the grandmothers of my generation.

The letters contained in this book are selected from women's requests for and responses to the Children's Bureau pamphlets from 1915 to 1932.[2] In the late 1910s and

1. Children's Bureau, U.S. Department of Labor, *Infant Care*, Publication No. 8 (Washington, D.C.: Government Printing Office, 1914). Children's Bureau, U.S. Department of Labor, *Prenatal Care*, Publication No. 4 (Washington, D.C.: Government Printing Office, 1913). Alice Taylor Ladd, Middletown, Conn., to Mrs. Max West, Sept. 15, 1917, File 8-6-2-0, Children's Bureau Records, Central Files, 1914–1940, Record Group 102, National Archives, Washington, D.C. (hereafter cited as CB).

2. The originals can be found in the Children's Bureau Records at the National Archives. The letters in this book are drawn primarily from the files on infant and maternal health (4-4) dated 1914–1920, 1921–1924, 1925–1928, and 1929–1932.

1920s, women from all over the United States flooded the
Children's Bureau, a division of the Department of Labor,
with their worries and questions about raising children.
They described the symptoms of sick children and asked advice about the diet, feeding schedules, discipline, and toilet
training of their babies. Some even sent along photographs
of their children or invited Bureau officials into their homes.

Initially distributed free of charge, *Prenatal Care* (1913)
and *Infant Care* (1914) quickly became government best
sellers. Between 1914 and 1921, almost 1,500,000 copies of
Infant Care were distributed. By 1929, the Children's Bureau estimated that one-half of U.S. babies had benefited
from the government's childrearing information.[3] In 1965,
the Department of Health, Education and Welfare (which
then housed the Children's Bureau) estimated that one
copy of the pamphlet, which has been published continuously since 1914, had been distributed for every three babies
born in the previous fifty years.[4] Written for the "average"
mother of the country, the bulletins circulated widely. They
were distributed by congressmen to their constituents and
shared among friends and relatives. Women from every
geographic region, social class, and educational background
wrote to the Bureau as many as 125,000 letters a year. The
many letters from working-class and farm mothers show that
the bulletins were read by the poor, many of whom sought

---

3. Children's Bureau, U.S. Department of Labor, *Promotion of the
Welfare and Hygiene of Maternity and Infancy for the Fiscal Year Ending June
30, 1929*, Publication No. 230 (Washington, D.C.: Government Printing Office, 1931), 21.

4. Children's Bureau, U.S. Department of Health, Education, and
Welfare, *The Story of Infant Care* (pamphlet), 1965, File 8-6-8 C437(1),
CB.

information about childrearing and had enough faith in the Children's Bureau to turn to it for advice.[5]

The letters that are presented in this book document the daily life of the average mother. Childbirth and childrearing have recently begun to attract the attention of historians, but we still know little about the lives of mothers who did not work outside the home, engage in political or charitable activities, or raise famous children.[6] Most of those who wrote in diaries or memoirs about being mothers

5. Most of the correspondence appears to come from native white women on farms and in small towns, although race and ethnicity are impossible to determine. As their letters illustrate, many poor and otherwise uneducated women could read and write well enough to correspond with the Children's Bureau. Unfortunately, the Bureau's cumbersome filing system makes impractical a quantitative analysis of the region, education, or ethnicity of the correspondents. Nancy Weiss, "Mother: The Invention of Necessity: Dr. Benjamin Spock's *Baby and Child Care,*" *American Quarterly* 29 (Winter 1977): 519–547, first drew my attention to the letters. Her sensitive analysis of the manuals and the letters is the most complete discussion of the correspondence to date.

6. Barbara Ehrenreich and Deirdre English, *For Her Own Good: 150 Years of the Experts' Advice to Women* (Garden City, N.Y.: Anchor Books, 1979); Susan Strasser, *Never Done: A History of American Housework* (New York: Pantheon, 1982), and Nancy Pottishman Weiss, "The Mother-Child Dyad Revisited: Perceptions of Mothers and Children in Twentieth-Century Childrearing Manuals," *Journal of Social Issues* 34 (1978): 29–45, all look at childrearing advice from a feminist perspective. Weiss, "Mother: The Invention of Necessity," examines the experience of mothers who read the advice. Mary Ryan, *Womanhood in America: From Colonial Times to the Present,* 2nd ed. (New York: New Viewpoints, 1979), analyzes the lives of working-class housewives, although she does not discuss motherhood per se. Sheila Rothman, *Woman's Proper Place: A History of Changing Ideals and Practices, 1870 to the Present* (New York: Basic Books, 1978), deals with public policy and motherhood. See Molly Ladd-Taylor, "Mother-Work: Ideology, Public Policy and the Mothers' Movement, 1890–1930" (Ph.D. diss., Yale University, in progress).

were middle class, were unusually well educated, and did not have to worry about a lack of resources. The information we have about the lives of working-class women is derived largely from the observations of social scientists and reformers; those who speak for themselves are usually activists who wish to make a political statement or women who have "risen" out of poverty.[7] In contrast, the Children's Bureau letters are from typical women, who tell how they feel about their work, health, and poverty. They express women's immediate concerns and reflect their daily experience.

Although mothers were not often thought to be working because they were not in the paid labor force, their correspondence shows that motherhood was indeed hard work. Women of every class and level of education worried about their babies' health and diet, struggled with indifferent husbands and callous doctors, and coped with inadequate medical care, but some faced the added burdens of poverty, isolation, and rural living conditions. Their letters testify to the tremendous spirit, wit, and resourcefulness with which women raised their children. We can see from the letters that most women's primary concern was survival; feeding their children, clothing them, and keeping them healthy were the mothers' major concerns. Although women of all classes sought and followed expert childrearing advice, economic conditions determined the way they brought up their children.

7. For example, *Maternity*, a collection of letters of English working-class mothers, originally published by the Women's Cooperative Guild in 1915, comprises statements by politically active leaders in the Guild. The book was part of their campaign to improve welfare and services for the family. Margaret Llewelyn Davies, ed., *Maternity* (New York: Norton, 1978).

Today we take for granted government health and welfare programs, but these programs did not exist for the
women who wrote to the Children's Bureau. Indeed, such
programs were the result in large measure of the efforts
of the Bureau staff (and the women's movement of which
these staff members were a part) to respond to the needs
and demands mothers expressed in their letters. These moving documents of women's lives motivated the agency staff
to develop welfare services. Along with the agency's responses, the letters illustrate women's role in the development of the U.S. welfare system. The Children's Bureau
designed and administered the first federal social-welfare
measure, the Sheppard-Towner Maternity and Infancy Protection Act of 1922. During the seven years of its operation, public health workers disseminated information on
nutrition and hygiene, established well-baby clinics, and
provided prenatal care for pregnant women in rural areas.
Sheppard-Towner was the model for the maternal and child
health provisions of the Social Security Act of 1935. The
Children's Bureau also lobbied for mothers' pensions (incorporated into the Social Security Act as Aid to Dependent Children) and for child-labor legislation, which became law in the Fair Labor Standards Act of 1937.[8]

The letters women wrote to the Children's Bureau reveal
that they desperately needed and wanted government aid
for their families. They show that many women felt entitled
to adequate health care and saw in the Bureau campaigns to
save babies a hopeful sign that the government was beginning to acknowledge their troubles and provide some com-

8. Lela Costin, *Two Sisters for Social Justice* (Urbana, Ill,: University
of Illinois Press, 1983).

pensation for motherhood. Today, as we are faced with reductions in welfare services and the elimination of many
of the programs that resulted from the Children's Bureau
efforts, these letters serve as an important reminder of
the conditions under which children were raised, and of
women's struggles, in the years before such services existed.

The Women
of the Children's Bureau

Established in 1912, the Children's Bureau was the brain-
child of Lillian Wald, the nurse and founder of the Henry
Street Settlement in New York City, and of child-labor activist Florence Kelley. Angered by a 1903 federal campaign
against the boll weevil while the deaths of 300,000 babies a
year brought no public outcry, Wald and Kelley proposed a
federal agency devoted to the welfare of children.[9] In 1910,
statistics were unavailable for most of the nation, but, in
states that did register births and deaths, 124 infants died
for every 1,000 live births. Children under five accounted
for one-quarter of all deaths, and mortality rates for blacks
were double those for whites. Death rates outside the states
with birth registration were even higher.[10]

---

9. Dorothy Bradbury, "The Children's Advocate: The Story of the
United States Children's Bureau, 1903–1946," n.d., Martha May Eliot
Papers, Arthur and Elizabeth Schlesinger Library on the History of
Women in America, Radcliffe College (hereafter cited as SL).
   10. Henry H. Hibbs, Jr., *Infant Mortality: Its Relation to Social and In-*

First introduced in Congress in 1906 with support from the National Child Labor Committee, the Children's Bureau bill received a major boost in 1909, when Theodore Roosevelt and participants at the White House Conference on the Care of Dependent Children endorsed the idea of a federal bureau that would address the "needs of children" throughout the United States.[11] The idea of a Children's Bureau was supported by women's clubs, parent-teacher associations, trade unions, and civic groups, but conservatives complained that child-caring work was a state responsibility and a waste of public funds. It took six years—and eleven bills—before the Children's Bureau was established.

Housed under the Department of Labor (it is today in the Administration for Children, Youth, and Families in the Department of Health and Human Services), the Children's Bureau was originally conceived of as a fact-finding agency. It was allocated $25,640 to "investigate and report upon all matters pertaining to the welfare of children and child life among all classes of our people," including infant

dustrial Conditions (New York: Russell Sage Foundation, 1916), 3–5. Bureau of the Census, U.S. Department of Commerce, Historical Statistics of the United States, Colonial Times to 1970, pt. I (Washington, D.C.: Government Printing Office, 1975), 57. See also Richard Alan Meckel, "The Awful Responsibility of Motherhood: American Health Reform and the Prevention of Infant and Child Mortality before 1913" (Ph.D. diss., University of Michigan, 1980).

11. Jacqueline Parker and Edward M. Carpenter, "Julia Lathrop and the Children's Bureau: The Emergence of an Institutions," Social Service Review 55 (Mar. 1981): 60. On the origins and early years of the Children's Bureau, see Nancy Pottishman Weiss, "Save the Children: A History of the Children's Bureau, 1903–1918" (Ph.D. diss., University of California at Los Angeles, 1974), and Louis J. Covotsos, "Child Welfare and Social Progress: A History of the United States Children's Bureau, 1912–1935" (Ph.D. diss., University of Chicago, 1976).

mortality, juvenile delinquency, illegitimacy, child labor, and mothers' pensions.[12]

"The first appropriation was small," Wald reflected, "but the first appointment was big."[13] Like other reformers who worked closely with the Children's Bureau, Wald credited its initial success to the first chief, Julia Lathrop. A long-time resident of Hull House with years of experience in the Illinois social services, Lathrop headed a mostly female staff of fifteen, which included *Infant Care* author Mary Mills West. With limited resources, she used her extensive contacts among members of women's clubs, college-educated women, social workers, and scholars to mobilize community support for child-welfare work.

Like the Bureau's second chief, Grace Abbott, Lathrop was a college graduate whose life revolved around a close-knit community of women in the social settlements. Both women came from midwestern families with an independent pioneer spirit and liberal ideas on women's rights and the abolition of slavery. Lathrop was born in Rockford, Illinois, in 1858, graduated from Vassar College, and moved to Hull House in 1890, shortly after it was founded. In Chicago she developed her lifelong interest in the welfare of children and the insane, whom she felt were powerless to protect themselves. While serving on the Illinois State Board of Charities, Lathrop urged separate facilities and professional care for the mentally ill and was instrumental in the establishment of the Cook County Juvenile Court in 1899. She was chief of the Children's Bureau from 1912 to

12. From the law establishing the Children's Bureau, quoted in *Prenatal Care*, 2.

13. Quoted in Bradbury, "The Children's Advocate," 58.

1921. After retiring from the Bureau, Lathrop served as president of the Illinois League of Women Voters and was appointed to the Child Welfare Committee of the League of Nations. She died in Rockford in 1932.[14]

A close friend of Jane Addams, Lathrop shared with the Hull House founder a genuine respect and sympathy for the poor (evident in her responses to mothers' letters) and a disdain for social conflict. Her interest in reform was motivated more by compassion than by any personal identification with the troubles of poor women. "The justice of today is born of yesterday's pity," she told the National Conference of Charities and Corrections in 1912.[15] Lathrop was remarkably sensitive to the problems of poor women, but her social-work perspective confined her solutions to professionally run welfare programs rather than to far-reaching change. Out of her own pocket she sent women money for food and clothing, yet she ignored their need for birth control. Lathrop advocated mothers' pensions and workmen's compensation for widowed and divorced women but thought that maternity insurance would be premature. Although she recommended that allowances be paid to all mothers as a temporary measure during the war, she believed that women's poverty would be eliminated when wages were sufficiently high for men to support their families while their wives stayed home with the children.[16]

14. Edward T. James, Janet Wilson James, and Paul Boyer, eds., *Notable American Women* (Cambridge, Mass.: Belknap Press, 1971), vol. 2, 370–372.

15. Quoted in Bradbury, "The Children's Advocate," 65.

16. Julia Lathrop, "Provision for the Care of the Families and Dependents of Soldiers and Sailors," *Proceedings of the Academy of Political Science* 7 (Feb. 1918): 796–807. Julia Lathrop to Mary O'Neill, Jan. 27,

Although Lathrop personally rejected marriage, she did
not question the idea that motherhood was "the most essential of employments." Like many other women reformers of her generation, she wanted to expand women's rights
but continued to believe that mothers should remain at
home with their children. Yet, despite her traditional con-
ception of women's responsibilities at home, Lathrop dis-
carded a sentimental view of women's nature. "Tenderness
and sympathy and adaptation . . . belong to choice individuals, and not to man or woman as such," she told the
Chicago Board of Charities.[17]

Like her mentor Lathrop, Grace Abbott lived at Hull
House for many years. A Nebraska native who moved to
Chicago in 1908, Abbott identified with the difficulties of
recent arrivals to the city. She helped found the Immigrants' Protective League, which aided the immigrants' ad-
justment to American life and sought to liberalize immigra-
tion laws. She was also active in the women's suffrage
movement and the 1911 Chicago garment workers' strike.
From 1916 until it was declared unconstitutional in 1918,
Abbott directed the enforcement of the federal child-labor
law for the Children's Bureau in Washington, D.C. After a
brief return to Chicago to head the Illinois State Immigra-
tion Commission, she was appointed chief of the Children's
Bureau in 1921. In 1934, Abbott retired from the Bureau

1917, File 10-471-28, CB. Lathrop's successor, Grace Abbott, also opposed maternity insurance. See Grace Abbott to Alida Malkus, Mar. 24,
1925, File 4-10-5, CB, and Grace Abbott to Dr. Willystine Goodsell,
Mar. 16, 1927, File 4-10-5, CB.

17. Julia Lathrop, "Highest Education for Women," *Journal of Home
Economics* 8 (Jan. 1916): 1–8. Quoted in Costin, *Two Sisters for Social
Justice*, viii.

but not from political activity. She served on the President's Council on Economic Security and helped draft the
children's sections of the 1935 Social Security Act. Upon
her return to the Midwest, Abbott became editor of the Social Service Review and professor of public welfare at the
University of Chicago School of Social Service Administration. She died in 1939.[18]

Other members of the Children's Bureau staff were
college-educated women who became involved in child-
welfare work because of their own experience. Infant Care
author Mary Mills West, a graduate of the University of
Minnesota, was a widowed mother of five who turned to
writing to support her family. Dorothy Reed Mendenhall,
Children's Bureau medical officer from 1917 to 1936, lost
two children before they were three years old, one of them
at birth. The author of the Bureau publications Milk: The
Indispensable Food for Children (1918) and Midwifery in Denmark (1929), which argued against unnecessary medical
interference in childbirth, Mendenhall also suffered from
puerperal sepsis as a result of bad obstetrics. Her grandmother too had died in childbirth.[19]

The women who worked with the Children's Bureau
were committed equally to their careers and to social re-

18. James, James, and Boyer, Notable American Women, vol. 1, 2–4;
Costin, Two Sisters for Social Justice, is an excellent biography of Grace
Abbott and her sister Edith.

19. Biographical information on West is available in Children's Bureau, The Story of Infant Care and in letters (such as Mary West to Mrs.
N.W., Washington, Mar. 16, 1920, File 4-10-5, CB.). On Mendenhall,
see Barbara Sicherman and Carol Hurd Green, eds., Notable American
Women: The Modern Period (Cambridge, Mass.: Belknap Press, 1980),
468–470, and Gena Corea, The Hidden Malpractice (New York: Morrow,
& Co. 1977), 185.

form. As women and mothers, they believed that they had
a unique ability and responsibility to further humanistic
goals. "Being women as well as physicians we share with
our sex in the actual and potential motherhood of the
race," said physician and child-welfare worker Florence
Sherbon. "Being women we make common cause with all
women as it is shown in our present affiliation with federate
clubs, etc. And being women and mothers, our first and
closest and dearest interest is the child."[20] Unlike feminists
today, women reformers in the 1910s considered the inter-
ests of women and children to be identical. They wanted
to expand women's rights but did not dream that women
could find fulfillment outside of motherhood. As nurses, social workers, and physicians, women professionals fulfilled
their maternal obligation to society by engaging in interesting and socially recognized (paid) work outside the home.

The Children's Bureau correspondence reveals the staff's
dual commitment to professionalism and reform. Although
their letters show a remarkable sensitivity to cultural and
class differences among women, they still reflect the staff's
middle-class values. For example, West wrote a long and
sympathetic letter to a woman who asked for help with her
household schedule, but wanted to "dismiss . . . from our
minds" another who rejected the help offered by social
workers. Lathrop's letters also demonstrate her particular
admiration for mothers who shared her faith in the value of
work and who expressed a distaste for charity. Just as distance and anonymity enabled poor women to turn to the
Bureau (a fact of which the Bureau staff was well aware), so
they allowed the agency staff to be more tolerant of poor

20. Quoted in Rothman, *Woman's Proper Place*, 140.

women than they might have been had they been in close touch with them personally.[21]

Despite its limitations, the Children's Bureau was a remarkable achievement. By involving thousands of women in the planning of social-service and government agencies, the Children's Bureau staff built an effective network of agencies that was unusually sensitive to the needs and wishes of the women it served. The Bureau effort to develop a prevention-oriented public health system run by women doctors and nurses greatly expanded women's influence in government, politics, and medicine. That women controlled a government agency even before they had won the vote is a testimony to the strength of the women's movement—and these individual women—in those years.

Women and Medical Care in the 1910s and 1920s

Today women preach the virtues of woman-controlled natural childbirth, but the letters contained in this book show

21. Mary West to Mrs. N.W., Washington, Mar. 16, 1920, File 4-10-5, CB. Mary West to Frances Etchberger, Baltimore Babies' Milk Fund Association, Apr. 24, 1918, File 4-4-3-2, CB. Julia Lathrop to Mrs. W.S., New York, Jan. 30, 1918, File 9-4-4-1, CB. Children's Bureau, U.S. Department of Labor, *Promotion of the Welfare and Hygiene of Maternity and Infancy for the Fiscal Year Ending June 30, 1925*, Publication No. 156 (Washington, D.C.: Government Printing Office, 1926), 13–14.

that their grandmothers usually dreaded the experience. Between 1900 and 1930, childbirth posed a serious threat to women's health: approximately sixty white and over one hundred nonwhite women died for every ten thousand live births; countless others suffered painful and disabling injuries. Indeed, some observers attributed the declining birth rate among educated white women to women's dread of childbirth. Some women, like Mrs. R.C. (whose letter appears in chapter 3), turned to birth control because of fear or a bad experience with childbirth.[22]

When they did have children, most women looked to science and medicine to help them give birth safely. Although figures varied according to region, class, and ethnicity, the number of women receiving medical care during confinement increased dramatically during the first three decades of the twentieth century. In 1915 the Children's Bureau found that nine-tenths of native white and one-half of foreign-born women interviewed in Waterbury, Connecticut, had been attended in childbirth by physicians. Of

22. Children's Bureau, U.S. Department of Labor, *Maternal Mortality*, Publication No. 158 (Washington, D.C.: Government Printing Office, 1926), 6. Judith Walzer Leavitt and Whitney Walton, "Down to Death's Door: Women's Perceptions of Childbirth in America," in Judith Walzer Leavitt, ed., *Women and Health in America* (Madison, Wis.: University of Wisconsin Press, 1984), 155–165. Joyce Antler and Daniel M. Fox, "The Movement toward a Safe Maternity: Physician Accountability in New York City, 1915–1940," in Judith Walzer Leavitt and Ronald Numbers, eds., *Sickness and Health in America* (Madison, Wis.: University of Wisconsin Press, 1978), 375–392. Richard W. Wertz and Dorothy C. Wertz, *Lying-In: A History of Childbirth in America* (New York: Free Press, 1977), analyzes changes in childbirth in the United States. See also Nancy Schrom Dye, "A History of Childbirth in America," *Signs* 6 (1980): 97–108. Mrs. R.C., Florida, to Children's Bureau, Jan. 27, 1932, File 4-5-7-3-1, CB.

the deliveries 10 percent (20 percent of those of native white women) had taken place in hospitals. In contrast, although four out of five white Mississippi mothers were attended by physicians between 1916 and 1918, 88 percent of the blacks had midwives. Only 1 of the 675 Mississippi mothers interviewed by the Children's Bureau had been confined in a hospital. Despite the growing popularity of medical care, many poor and immigrant women continued to employ midwives because they wanted to be attended by women, because midwives helped with housework, and because they were cheaper: while doctors in Waterbury generally charged $15 to $25, midwives charged only $8. Nevertheless, between 1900 and 1930 the national percentage of births attended by midwives dropped from 50 to 15 percent.[23]

Although hospital births were out of reach for most women, middle-class women in the cities increasingly chose to have their children in a hospital. In 1900, less than 5 percent of U.S. mothers gave birth in a hospital; not quite forty years later, between 60 and 75 percent of urban women—and half of all women—delivered their babies in a hospital.[24] Although hospital birth was supposed to offer safe, sanitary, round-the-clock care, and a chance to escape

23. Children's Bureau, U.S. Department of Labor, *Infant Mortality: Results of a Field Study in Waterbury, Conn., Based on Births in One Year*, Publication No. 29 (Washington, D.C.: Government Printing Office, 1918), 45–48. Children's Bureau, U.S. Department of Labor, *Maternity and Child Care in Selected Rural Areas of Mississippi*, Publication No. 88 (Washington, D.C.: Government Printing Office, 1921), 27, 21. Judy Barrett Litoff, *American Midwives, 1860 to the Present* (Westport, Conn.: Greenwood Press, 1978), 58.

24. Wertz, *Lying-In*, 133.

from housework, women's letters document that it remained a dangerous and unpleasant experience. The use of forceps and drugs (more common in hospitals than at home) added to women's discomfort and often complicated their recovery.

Although instrumental and drug-induced deliveries often seriously endangered mother and child, women continued to idealize science and medicine. In the 1910s and 1920s, large numbers of upper-class women, many of them feminists, urged their doctors to deliver their babies while they were under the influence of the narcotic scopolamine, or twilight sleep. Ironically, they had to fight with male physicians who opposed the drug and who objected to women's attempt to decide what kind of delivery they would have.[25] The letters to the Children's Bureau and the twilight-sleep movement demonstrate that terror of natural childbirth led women to accept—and even demand—medical intervention in the birth process. However, women's search for safe childbirth contributed in the end to their loss of control over the birth experience.

Just as middle-class women turned to medicine to help them escape painful childbirth, they also looked to doctors for guidance on infant feeding. Poor diet was a major cause of infant illness and mortality, especially in the hot summer months. Yet, although maternal breastfeeding was considered the most important factor in reducing mortality due to gastrointestinal disease, the number of women who bottle-fed their babies increased between 1870 and 1930. Like the

25. Judith Walzer Leavitt, "Birthing and Anesthesia: The Debate over Twilight Sleep," in Leavitt, *Women and Health in America*, 175–184. Several women requested information on twilight sleep from the Children's Bureau; see File 4-4-3-4 (1921–1924), CB.

use of physicians, feeding practices varied according to culture and ethnicity. Middle-class white women, who most often employed doctors during delivery, were also the most frequent users of artificial infant formula. The shift from breastfeeding to bottlefeeding resulted from the growth of commercial and infant food manufacturers, the availability of pure milk, the rise of pediatrics as a medical specialty, and the changing role of women. A medically authorized, "scientific" substitute for breast milk, artificial infant formula enabled women to continue their activities outside the home without fear that they would harm their children.[26] Along with physician-attended and hospital births, the increase in bottlefeeding added to the influence and prestige of physicians.

The Campaign
to Save the Babies

Because the Children's Bureau mandate did not allow it to provide direct aid or medical services, Lathrop was forced to rely on public education to achieve her goal of adequate

26. Rima Apple, "To Be Used Only under the Direction of a Physician: Commercial Infant Feeding and Medical Practice, 1870–1940," *Bulletin of the History of Medicine* 54 (Fall 1980): 402–417, discusses the relationship between doctors and businesses in developing infant formulas. Kathy Jones, "Sentiment and Science: The Late 19th Century Pediatrician as Mother's Advisor," *Journal of Social History* (Fall 1983): 79–96, examines women's acceptance of medical advice.

medical and prenatal care for all women. The Children's
Bureau staff hoped that its child-care bulletins, birth registration campaign, and research into the causes and extent
of infant and maternal mortality would lead women to demand the health care to which they were entitled. Replying
to Mrs. R.P., who suffered a miscarriage because she had no
medical aid, Children's Bureau physician Florence Kraker
wrote, "The importance of prenatal care has not until quite
recently been fully realized by the medical profession as well
as the general public. . . . That women realize and appreciate the need of prenatal care is a great factor in developing
the service rendered."[27]

Although the initial sponsors of the Children's Bureau
had been child-labor activists, Lathrop determined that the
agency could build public support best by focusing its limited resources initially on researching infant mortality
rather than on the more controversial subject of child labor. Reflecting the priorities of Progressive reform, the Bureau publishing and research projects were geared toward
action. Lathrop's cautious research strategy, careful development of contacts in local communities, and public rela-
tions campaign led to tremendous public support for the
agency and paved the way for comprehensive programs. In
1914, the Children's Bureau received funding six and one-
half times greater than its original appropriation.[28] As funding for the Bureau grew, so did its responsibilities. The
agency enforced the federal child-labor law from 1916 until

27. Florence Kraker to Mrs. R.P., Iowa, Feb. 26, 1924, File 4-4-2-2,
CB.
    28. Parker and Carpenter, "Julia Lathrop and the Children's Bu-
reau," 63–65. Bradbury, "The Children's Advocate," 82.

it was declared unconstitutional two years later, and it administered the Sheppard-Towner Act from 1922 until funds ran out in 1929. Throughout its first two decades, the Bureau worked with women's groups, community organizations, physicians, and state health departments to disseminate information on child care and to win public support for its baby-saving campaign.

Even the Children's Bureau studies of infant mortality were orchestrated with the help of the community. Lathrop worked with women's clubs, civic groups, the press, and the clergy to lay the groundwork for the Bureau's 1913 study of infant mortality in Johnstown, Pennsylvania. With local women acting as interpreters, only 2 of the 1,553 mothers visited refused to be interviewed.[29] Because the Children's Bureau considered mortality to be a social and economic rather than a medical or moral problem, the interviews focused on hygiene and economics, including feeding practices, housing conditions, neighborhood sanitation and sewage, and income.

Not surprisingly, the results of the investigation reflected Progressive reformers' environmental and educational priorities. The Children's Bureau investigators found a striking correlation between infant mortality and poverty. A child whose father earned under $521 a year was almost twice as likely to die as one whose father earned over $1,200, and infant deaths increased by 40 percent when homes did not have running water. According to Lathrop,

29. Children's Bureau, U.S. Department of Labor, *Infant Mortality: Results of a Field Study in Johnstown, Pa., Based on Births in One Year*, Publication No. 9 (Washington, D.C.: Government Printing Office, 1915), 6.

infant mortality was caused by "a coincidence of underpaid fathers, overworked and ignorant mothers, and those hazards to the life of the offspring which individual parents cannot avoid or control because they must be remedied by community action." [30]

In seven subsequent studies, investigators found much the same result: most infant deaths were preventable. Gastrointestinal disease (the major cause of infant mortality in Johnstown) resulted from poor nutrition and feeding and was easily reduced by maternal breastfeeding and education. Respiratory disease was attributed to overcrowded and unsanitary conditions, and the diseases of early infancy were considered a result largely of inadequate prenatal care. The results of all the studies were widely publicized in newspaper and magazine articles, in speeches, and at conferences.

The publicity accorded the Children's Bureau investigations and projects led growing numbers of women to become involved in its activities. In 1914 the agency reported that 1,500 club women in seventeen states helped with its campaign for birth registration; during Children's Year, just four years later, an estimated eleven million women served on more than seventeen thousand committees. The Bureau worked closely with women's organizations, such as the General Federation of Women's Clubs, to develop National Baby Week, which began in 1916. The second year of World War I, 1918, was designated Children's Year, and the Children's Bureau, along with the Women's Committee of the Council of National Defense, received a special appropriation. In order to publicize a standard of normal child development, Bureau volunteers systematically weighed and measured the nation's children. Six and one-half mil-

30. Ibid., 53, 22.

lion preschool children in more than 16,500 cities, towns, and rural communities were examined during Children's Year.[31]

One year later—and just ten years after the 1909 White House conference at which the Children's Bureau was born—the agency organized a second White House conference on children. Club women, physicians, economists, and social workers together planned the 1919 conference on the Minimum Standards of Child Welfare. The conference concluded that medical, nursing, and hospital care should be universally available, "as the public schools are, . . . to be used by all with dignity and self-respect." Examinations, instruction, care during confinement, and follow-up for six weeks after delivery by a doctor, nurse, or "properly trained attendant" should be provided by prenatal or maternity centers to any woman not receiving care from a private physician. In addition, the conference advised that women should have ten days rest and household help for at least four weeks after a normal delivery. Finally, it recommended that allowances be paid to the wives and children of soldiers and sailors and that mothers receive an income sufficient to allow them to remain at home while they were nursing. "Let us not deceive ourselves," Lathrop said in another speech the same year. "The power to maintain a decent family living standard is the primary essential of child welfare. This means a living wage and wholesome working life for the man, a good and skillful mother at home to keep the house and comfort all within it. Society can afford no less and can afford no exception."[32]

31. Grace Abbott, "Ten Years' Work for Children," *North American Review* 218 (Aug. 1923): 189–200.

32. Quoted in Bradbury, "The Children's Advocate," 113–115, 109.

The female orientation and reform perspective of the Children's Bureau put it in conflict with some members of the medical profession. West was hurt when the Medical Advisory Committee, which had been established in 1919 to help with the revisions of *Infant Care*, insisted that her name be removed from the bulletins because she was not a physician. Upset at the "injustice" of the committee's attitude that only physicians were experts on childrearing, she wrote that she had borne five children, and "as I am not a hopelessly feeble-minded woman, I must have learned a few things for myself by that process." When the committee tried to remove discussion of "diagnosis, treatment and etiology of disease" from the bulletins, Mendenhall fumed to Lathrop: "Personally I believe mothers have a right to know the scientific reasons which underlie infant feeding and that the mothers our bulletins reach are capable of understanding such information. The farmers of our country are educated by bulletins from the Department of Agriculture in regard to infectious diseases. . . . Why then, should references to marasmus and scurvy and their treatment, which often result from improper feeding in infancy, be cut out of a bulletin sent to mothers by the U.S. Children's Bureau?" [33]

Mendenhall prevailed in the 1921 revisions, but, by the end of the 1920s, the medical perspective had triumphed even within the Children's Bureau. The scientific and professional authority of medicine was so powerful—and doctors' criticism of the women-run maternal and child health

33. West quoted in Children's Bureau, *The Story of Infant Care*, 21. Dorothy Reed Mendenhall to Julia Lathrop, Nov. 12, 1920, File 8-6-2-2-3, CB.

programs of the Children's Bureau so effective—that the Bureau itself began to rely almost exclusively on medical solutions to women's health problems. Although the 1914 and 1921 editions of *Infant Care* had been written by West, the 1929 revision was directed by physician Martha Eliot, later the fourth chief of the Children's Bureau. By the end of the 1920s, "consult a physician" was the almost exclusive recommendation the Bureau staff made to the mothers who wrote them.

The final blow to the women reformers of the Children's Bureau occurred at the 1930 White House Conference on Child Health and Protection. Although club women played a major role at the 1919 White House Conference on Child Welfare Standards, the 1930 conference was geared toward medical specialists who opposed the Children's Bureau concept of entitlement to federally funded health care. Abbott, who had been the secretary of the 1919 conference, was given only a minor role in 1930. Over the vigorous objection of the friends of the Children's Bureau, the conference recommended a Hoover administration plan that would transfer future maternal and infant health programs from the Children's Bureau (a division of the Department of Labor) to the medically run Public Health Service. Although women reformers managed to stop this bill from becoming law, it signaled the end of an era.[34]

34. Costin, *Two Sisters for Social Justice,* 168–179. Rothman, *Woman's Proper Place,* 152–153. White House Conference on Child Health and Protection, *Official Proceedings* (New York: American Child Health Association, 1930).

The Maternity and
Infancy Protection Act

The influence of the Children's Bureau culminated with
the administration of the Sheppard-Towner Maternity and
Infancy Protection Act from 1922 to 1929. The legislation,
which provided federal matching grants to the states for
public health nurses, clinics, and instruction in maternal
and infant hygiene, was motivated in part by letters from
mothers like Mrs. A.P. (whose description of the difficulty
of obtaining prenatal care appears in chapter 1). Moved by
the arduous lives and courage of rural women, Lathrop designed a bill to provide women in remote areas with access
to the health care to which she felt they were entitled.[35]

The "mothers' bill" became a legislative priority of organized women. Introduced in 1918 in the House of Representatives by Jeannette Rankin, the first congresswoman, it
was endorsed by the National League of Women Voters, the
National Congress of Mothers and Parent-Teacher Associations, the National Council of Jewish Women, and the
Daughters of the American Revolution. Women flooded
their congressmen with petitions and letters about the
benefits of the "wonderful" bill. The Democratic, Socialist,
and Farmer-Labor parties supported the legislation, and

35. Mrs. A.P., Wyoming, to Julia Lathrop, Oct. 19, 1916, File
4-3-0-3, CB. I have reprinted only two of the many letters between
Lathrop and Mrs. A.P.

magazines such as *Good Housekeeping* went on vigorous promotional campaigns. Nevertheless, it was three years before the bill (then sponsored by Senator Morris Sheppard of Texas and Congressman Horace Towner of Iowa) was signed into law.[36] Proponents of the legislation asserted that high maternal and infant death rates betrayed the low value society placed on women's and children's lives. Congressmen who legislated salary and pension increases for postal employees and veterans claimed that the government did not have the money to fund health care for women and children. "No woman in the United States would begrudge those increases of salaries," Florence Kelley testified in congressional hearings, "but when we are told that this country is so poor and this Congress so harassed by things of greater importance than the deaths of a quarter of a million of children a year, . . . we say to ourselves, 'Surely we are not to take this seriously? . . . Why does Congress wish women and children to die?'"[37]

Although the bill was supported by the Medical Women's Association, the Child Health Association, and some pediatricians, the medical establishment opposed the measure. The American Medical Association feared that the prevention-oriented Sheppard-Towner Act would lead to

36. J. Stanley Lemons, *The Woman Citizen: Social Feminism in the 1920s* (Urbana, Ill.: University of Illinois Press, 1975), 153–180. Joseph Chepaitis, "The First Federal Social Welfare Measure: The Sheppard-Towner Maternity and Infancy Act, 1918–1932" (Ph.D. diss., Georgetown University, 1968).

37. House Committee on Interstate and Foreign Commerce, *Public Protection of Maternity and Infancy: Hearings on H.R. 10925*, 66th Cong., 3d sess., Dec. 21, 1920, 28.

state medicine. Its members maintained that, if passed, the act should be administered by the doctors of the Public Health Service rather than by the social workers and women physicians at the Children's Bureau. At first, the Children's Bureau staff dismissed their opponents as "a reactionary group of medical men who are not progressive and have no public health point of view."[38] "We are not treating sick people," Dr. S. Josephine Baker, director of the New York City Bureau of Child Hygiene, insisted in congressional hearings. "We simply teach people how to keep well and readjust as far as we are able the bad effects of wrong environment. . . . In fact, mortality is very largely a social problem and an economic problem."[39] There was little reason for doctors to object.

Conservative groups such as the National Association Opposed to Woman Suffrage also opposed maternity and infancy aid. Glorifying maternal instinct, opponents of the Sheppard-Towner Act asserted that mother love was all women needed to raise healthy children. They believed that the scientific information on child care from the Children's Bureau was an insult to American motherhood, and they attributed the large number of infant deaths to modern women's "distaste for the obligations and pains of maternity" (as one congressman put it). They claimed that the maternity and infancy legislation would promote birth control, illegitimacy, bolshevism, and government control of

38. Anna Rude, quoted in Rothman, *Woman's Proper Place*, 138. See also Lemons, *The Woman Citizen*, 162–167.

39. House Committee on Interstate and Foreign Commerce, *Public Protection of Maternity and Infancy: Hearings on H.R. 2366*, 67th Cong., 1st sess., July 12, 1921, 21.

children. Conservative opponents of the legislation tried to turn mothers (like Mrs. L.G. whose letter appears in chapter 3) against the act by publicizing the fact that its authors were unmarried. According to conservative Senator James Reed, the real purpose of the bill was to allow "a few single ladies holding Government jobs at Washington" to teach the nation's mothers how to raise their children. Instead, he sarcastically proposed legislation that would teach the Bureau staff "how to acquire a husband and have babies of their own."[40]

Despite the opposition of doctors and conservatives, the Sheppard-Towner Act passed by a wide margin on November 23, 1921. Suffragists and women reformers considered Sheppard-Towner—the first "women's bill" to pass Congress since they had won the vote—a great victory and proof that women's participation in politics would improve the nation's welfare. "Of all the activities in which I have shared during more than forty years of striving, none is, I am convinced, of such fundamental importance as the Sheppard-Towner act," Kelley declared.[41] Nevertheless, the actual provisions of the bill were modest. It provided $1,480,000 for 1922 and $1,240,000 for each of the next five years to be distributed as matching funds to the states and used for instruction in maternal and child hygiene. Although states could (and did) gather statistics, train and license practicing midwives, hold conferences and classes for

40. *Congressional Record*, vol. 61, 67th Cong., 1st sess., Nov. 1, 1921, 7148. Mrs. L.G., Pennsylvania, to Grace Abbott, Apr. 11, 1922, File 11-40-2, CB. *Congressional Record*, vol. 61, 67th Cong., 1st sess., July 21, 1921, 8764.
41. Quoted in Lemons, *The Woman Citizen*, 155.

new mothers, and distribute literature—including the popular correspondence courses for pregnant women—the law forbade outright aid or medical care. It expressly denied government agents the right to enter a home uninvited and gave individuals the right to refuse aid.

Notwithstanding the modesty of its provisions, the Sheppard-Towner Act had a significant impact on women's and children's health. Although each state had to pass special legislation before it could receive funds, eventually only Massachusetts, Connecticut, and Illinois declined government aid. In seven years Sheppard-Towner agents distributed over twenty-two million pieces of literature, conducted 183,252 health conferences, established 2,978 permanent prenatal centers, and visited over three million homes. Thirty-one states established midwife training programs.[42] Several southwestern states held prenatal classes in Spanish, and the Minnesota Division of Child Hygiene hired two public health nurses who spoke the Indian language Chippewa. County nurses traveled by car and by horseback, climbed over mountains and across creeks to visit sick mothers and infants who lived in remote areas and had no other medical or prenatal care. In Alabama, Sheppard-Towner funds increased the percentage of the population with access to health care from 43 percent in 1922 to 82 percent in 1929.[43]

Although the numbers can be misleading because several

42. *Promotion of the Welfare . . . 1929*, 27.
43. "Division of Child Hygiene Activities," enclosed in E.C. Hartley to Dorothy Kirchwey Brown, Mar. 5, 1929, Box 2, Folder 44, and Jessie Mariner to Dorothy Kirchwey Brown, Mar. 5, 1929, Box 2, Folder 38, Dorothy Kirchwey Brown Papers, SL. In her capacity as head of the child-welfare committee of the National League of Women Voters, Brown obtained a number of state reports on the progress of Sheppard-

states with high infant and maternal death rates were in-cluded in the figures for the first time during the 1920s, the achievements of the Sheppard-Towner Act are evident in the statistics. Maternal deaths rose slightly (from sixty-eight per ten thousand births in 1921 to sixty-nine in 1929), but mortality in rural areas—where the act focused—declined from fifty-nine to fifty-six per ten thousand births. The na-tional infant death rate declined from seventy-six per thou-sand live births in 1921 to sixty-nine in 1928. In states that were in the birth-registration area throughout the operation of Sheppard-Towner, infant mortality declined by 11 per-cent. Deaths due to gastrointestinal disease dropped 47 per-cent. In the first five years of the act, infant mortality among blacks decreased from 110 to 100 deaths per 1,000 live births. The Children's Bureau estimated that Sheppard-Towner funds saved the lives of sixty thousand babies.[44]

The accomplishments of the Sheppard-Towner Act are documented in the letters of appreciation received by the state directors who administered the programs. "I can no-tice in my obstetrical work year after year that the general knowledge of infant care and prenatal care and general hygiene is decidedly on the increase," attested one Colo-rado doctor. "It has become a very rare thing to have a call on a confinement case at the onset of labor without having seen the patient before." "I trust you'll find by many letters that your work is doing much and will continue it," wrote a

---

Towner activities. The monthly reports from state child hygiene depart-ments to the Children's Bureau are in File 11-0, CB.

44. Children's Bureau, *Promotion of the Welfare . . .* 1929, 28–34. During the course of Sheppard-Towner, the number of states included in the birth registration area increased from the District of Columbia and twenty-seven states to forty-five states, the District of Columbia, and the territory of Hawaii.

West Virginia mother of twins. "There are many who do
not Pay attention But It Is a great Benefit to those that do. I
could not get along with out your helpful pamphlets and
Bulletins." A New York woman added, "When people stop
me on the street and ask the whys and wherefores of my so
obviously healthy baby I always say 'He's a Government
baby,' giving all credit to your bulletin (Infant Care). I was
lucky enough not to know anything about babies before and
not to have any relatives who thought they did." And a
Georgia mother agreed, "We are so glad the day has come
when we have someone to care for our babies when they get
sick."[45]

Despite the popularity of the legislation among rural
mothers and the modesty of its provisions, conservatives
and the medical establishment marshaled their resources to
defeat the Sheppard-Towner Act when appropriations were
to be renewed in 1927. After a bitter struggle, supporters of
the bill agreed to a compromise that extended appropriations for two years but repealed the act automatically on June
30, 1929. After their attempts to reintroduce Sheppard-
Towner failed, the friends of the Children's Bureau found
themselves forced to oppose an administration-backed plan

45. Dr. E. H. Munro, Mesa County, Colorado, to Mrs. Estelle Math-
ews, Colorado Child Welfare Bureau, Mar. 18, 1926, File 11-7-1. CB.
West Virginia Division of Child Hygiene and Public Health Nursing,
"Extracts from Statements of Mothers Who Took Motherhood Correspondence Course," enclosed in Katharine Lenroot to Julia Lathrop,
Sept. 23, 1926, File 11-0, CB. New York mother quoted in Children's
Bureau, U.S. Department of Labor, *Promotion of the Welfare and Hygiene
of Maternity and Infancy for the Fiscal Year Ending June 30, 1928*, Publication No. 194 (Washington, D.C.: Government Printing Office, 1929),
35. "Letters of Georgia Women Attending Prenatal Clinic," enclosed in
Joe Bowdoin to Dorothy Kirchwey Brown, Apr. 30, 1929, Box 2, Folder
39, Dorothy Kirchwey Brown Papers, SL.

that would renew maternity and infancy aid under the administration of the Public Health Service. Anticommunist attacks on Sheppard-Towner supporters, including Abbott and Kelley, and the disorganization of the women's movement in the post-suffrage years had weakened the effectiveness of the women's reform lobby. At the same time, the prosperity of the 1920s, the decline of the Progressive reform spirit, and the growing influence of physicians made government intervention in health care seem unnecessary and undesirable to the middle class. The Sheppard-Towner Act had motivated doctors to incorporate preventive care into their practices, but the shift from public clinics to private care that resulted from the withdrawal of federal funds meant that such care was available only to women who could afford—and lived near—physicians. Although sixteen states tried to continue to provide significant maternity and infancy aid, the removal of federal funds severely reduced public support for the program. By 1934, fourteen states allocated less than $3,000 each to maternal and infant health care.[46]

A new administration restored some maternity and infancy aid in the Social Security Act of 1935. Although Abbott resigned from the Children's Bureau in 1934, she served on the Council on Economic Security and helped formulate the children's sections of the Social Security Act. With Katharine Lenroot and Martha Eliot, the third and fourth directors of the Children's Bureau, Abbott designed a four-point plan for children's aid that included a revised and extended system of maternal and child health care on the model of the Sheppard-Towner Act; welfare services for

46. Children's Bureau, *Promotion of the Welfare . . .* 1929, 39. Bradbury, "The Children's Advocate," 372.

homeless, dependent, and neglected children; crippled children's services; and aid to dependent children. Although the Children's Bureau administered the first three programs, to Abbott's great disappointment Aid to Dependent Children was administered by the Social Security Administration.[47]

The Children's Bureau regained some of its old influence under the Roosevelt administration, but physicians and psychologists now defined the direction of child-welfare work. Their medical perspective replaced the earlier Children's Bureau model of community involvement in maternal and infant health care. There was little place for club women and social activists—or even women physicians— in the new work of the Bureau. Although all but three of the forty-eight state directors of child-welfare programs had been women when Sheppard-Towner began in 1922, by 1939 three-quarters of them were men.[48] Professionalism had triumphed over social reform.

Prenatal Care *and* Infant Care

Since West wrote the first edition of *Infant Care* in 1914, the bulletin has been revised twelve times. West herself revised the 1921 edition, but, beginning in 1929 (when *Infant Care* was completely rewritten to reflect the influence of behaviorist psychology), the authors were physicians.[49]

47. Costin, *Two Sisters for Social Justice*, 218–226.
48. S. Josephine Baker, *Fighting for Life* (New York: Macmillan, 1939), 201.
49. West was also the author of the 1913 edition of *Prenatal Care*. The 1930 revision of *Prenatal Care* was directed by physicians and re-

Thus, in the 1910s and 1920s women read the bulletins written by West, a mother who combined scientific advice with an implicit call for reform—for pure milk, sunshine, and fresh air to be made available to all children. In *Prenatal Care* and *Infant Care*, West incorporated the medical information contained in Dr. Luther Emmett Holt's popular *The Care and Feeding of Children* with motherly common sense, practical information, and time-saving tips.[50] Her blend of medical advice and hints on furnishing a nursery and preparing a layette reflected West's—and the Children's Bureau's—perception that infant health and welfare depended on much more than medicine.

Infant Care considered doctors and mothers to be partners in child health. Although Lathrop wrote in her introduction that the Children's Bureau did not intend to "invade the field of the medical or nursing professions" by publishing the child-care bulletin, she insisted that "every mother has a right to possess" information regarding hygiene.[51] West too warned her readers (and reassured doctors) that the medical information and suggested treatments of minor illnesses contained in *Infant Care* were not intended to "substitute for the care and advice of a physician" but were intended for women who lived far from medical care or who were faced with an emergency.[52] That West was not a doctor but a university-trained writer and

flected the influence of behaviorism. See Children's Bureau, U.S. Department of Labor, *Child Management*, Publication No. 143 (Washington, D.C.: Government Printing Office, 1925), for another example of a childrearing pamphlet influenced by behaviorism.

50. Luther Emmett Holt, *The Care and Feeding of Children. A Catechism for the Use of Mothers and Children* (New York: D. Appleton & Co., 1894).

51. *Infant Care* (1914), 7. Also in *Prenatal Care* (1913), 6.

52. *Infant Care* (1914), 63.

mother of five was in keeping with the Bureau belief that children's health did not depend primarily on medicine.

The early Children's Bureau pamphlets reflect the combination of science, efficiency, and sentiment that characterized the Progressive Era women's movement. West did not question the biological basis of women's role in the home, but she did believe that motherhood was a profession that required education and planning. She attributed infants' mental and physical deficiencies to inadequate training and poor environment rather than to heredity or nature, and believed that the mother should teach her child to replace natural impulses with the self-control and discipline assured by regular habits. According to West, good habits and a regular schedule would ease the child's transition to adulthood and make the mother's work easier. "The care of a baby is readily reduced to a system unless he is sick," she wrote. "Such a system is not only one of the greatest factors in keeping the baby well and in training him in a way which will be of value to him all through life, but reduces the work of the mother to a minimum and provides for her certain periods of rest and recreation."[53] West's emphasis on habit training and efficiency fit with the needs of an industrial society that was structured increasingly by the clock.

The first Children's Bureau pamphlet, *Prenatal Care*, was a call for women to take care of themselves during pregnancy. According to the agency, 70 percent of the infants who died before they were one month old did so as a result of inadequate prenatal conditions or birth injury.[54] *Prenatal*

53. Ibid., 59.
54. *Prenatal Care* (1913), 5.

Care covered the range of information an expectant mother needed to know: personal hygiene, avoiding the complications of pregnancy, preparing for confinement and childbirth, and tips on outfitting, nursing, and caring for a newborn.

Disagreeing with the old superstition that sickness was a necessary accompaniment of pregnancy, West insisted that a healthy, well-rested mother was the best guarantee for a healthy child. She kindly but firmly disputed the widespread belief that a pregnant woman could injure or "mark" her child by seeing a deformed person or animal, or by encountering tragedy. The only way a woman might harm her unborn child was not in such a "fortuitous, accidental manner," West insisted. It was, rather, by her failure to care for herself and to "order her own life in the way that will result in the highest degree of health and happiness for herself and, therefore, for the child."[55]

As today, pregnant women were advised to eat good food, to sleep eight hours, to get plenty of rest and outdoor exercise, and to bathe every day. They were to guard against constipation by eating a moderate diet that consisted of very little meat, lots of green vegetables, and plenty of fluids, and to reduce their consumption of coffee, tea, and alcohol. West advised expectant mothers to wear comfortable dress and to replace their regular corsets with special maternity undergarments early in pregnancy. Heavy work, such as washing or sweeping, and strenuous exercise, including skating or dancing, were to be avoided. West's advice for the prevention and cure of the complications of pregnancy (such as hemorrhoids, morning sickness, and even miscar-

55. Ibid., 17; 20.

riage) was much the same: expectant mothers should not worry, but stay happy, eat and exercise in moderation, and be in regular consultation with a doctor. When it came to maternal and infant health, the advice for mother and child was the same.

In keeping with the Children's Bureau faith in medical care, West recommended hospital births over home delivery because they were safer, cheaper (there was no nurse's salary), and provided a respite from housework. However, in contrast to recent editions of *Prenatal Care*, which describe what will happen at the hospital, the many pages West devoted to supplies for home birth and ideas on reducing the cost of confinement suggest that she did not expect most women to deliver at a hospital.[56] The detailed discussions of labor pains, care of the newborn, nursing the baby, making baby clothes, and preparing a layette must have comforted women who lived far from medical care and were unsure about what to expect during confinement, but they may also have heightened the anxiety of those who had neither the resources nor the familial support to ensure adequate health care at home. At the same time, the middle-class standard of living assumed in the bulletins may have raised women's expectations about the care to which they were entitled.

Like *Prenatal Care*, *Infant Care* combined scientific advice with common sense and promoted the Progressive belief that maternal instinct alone was not sufficient to raise healthy babies. From how to lift the baby to how to make the baby's bed, no detail was too trivial for the pamphlet.

56. See U.S Department of Health, Education and Welfare, *Prenatal Care* (Washington, D.C.: Government Printing Office, 1973).

Because "an experienced mother is often greatly at a loss to
know whether a baby is properly thriving," West even listed
the signs of a healthy child, including clear skin, the ab-
sence of vomiting, and "no evidence of pain or discomfort!"[57] Reflecting the Bureau belief in the welfare of the
whole child, the bulletin included forms for birth registration and recording the baby's weight, recipes, charts of normal development, sample feeding schedules, patterns for
baby clothes, notes on how to choose and decorate the nursery, as well as symptoms of illness and instructions on caring for an ill child.

Because of the Progressive focus on the environment, the
bulletin began with instructions on the child's surroundings
and a plea that all babies live near open air and adequate
sanitation. Although she recognized that housing choices
were "usually limited" by family income, West maintained
that dark tenements were "not fit" homes for children and
suggested that houses in the suburbs or close to parks gave
city children "the best chance for proper growth and development."[58] In order to guard against respiratory disease,
one of the leading causes of infant mortality, she advised
that the baby's room be light and sunny, easily cleaned, and
well ventilated.

The industrial language and reliance on a combination of
science and nature that were characteristic of the Progressive Era are seen most clearly in the discussion of feeding.
Citing statistics that showed that nine-tenths of infant illness resulted from improper feeding, West described digestion as an "intricate operation" that required "complicated

57. *Infant Care* (1914), 51–52.
58. Ibid., 9.

machinery" (the digestive organs) to function properly. The 1980 edition of *Infant Care* advises feeding on demand, but West considered feeding by the clock to be the best way "to accustom the infant organs to do their work properly" as well as to make the mother's work easier. Because good digestion was necessary for the "growth, maintenance and repair of the body" and breast milk protected the baby from illness, West advised the nursing mother to keep her infant at the breast for twenty minutes every three or four hours (as the doctor advised). Babies were to be weighed regularly to see whether they were eating enough.[59] West considered nursing by the clock easier for mothers as well as safer for their children. It enabled women to establish a regular schedule for household chores and meant that no bottles had to be sterilized and no complicated formula prepared. However, the many pages devoted to sample formulas and instructions on preparing and sterilizing bottles suggest that many women bottlefed their babies.[60]

Although physicians in both the 1910s and the 1980s recommend breastfeeding, the advice concerning diet for older children has changed considerably. The 1980 edition of *Infant Care* encourages mothers to start babies on juice, vegetables, and cereal after several months, and to feed them (mashed) the food eaten by the rest of the family when they are nine or ten months old. In contrast, the first *Infant Care* did not introduce juice until the baby was seven

59. *Infant Care* (1914), 31–32. Office of Human Development Services, Administration for Children, Youth, and Families, U.S. Department of Health and Human Services, *Infant Care* (Washington, D.C.: Government Printing Office, 1980), 3–6.
60. On the transition to bottlefeeding, see Apple, "To Be Used Only under the Direction of a Physician."

or eight months old. Solid foods, other than a soft egg or toast, were not to be given at all during the first year. According to West, children should eat a simple diet consisting of beef juice, coddled eggs, toast, fruit juice, mild vegetables, cereals, and a quart of milk a day after they were weaned from the breast or bottle (between nine months and one year). Rich and fried foods, pastry, and sugars were to be avoided.[61]

A baby with a healthy diet is supposed to have regular bowel movements, and both the 1914 and the 1980 editions of *Infant Care* describe the color and texture of normal stools. Today bowel training does not normally begin until the child is almost two years old (and is not even mentioned in the 1980 edition of *Infant Care*), but in the 1910s women were urged to begin toilet training when the baby was three months old. Early toilet training would eliminate dirty diapers, which both bred disease and added considerably to the laundry. West recommended that the mother toilet train her infant by presenting the chamber pot to the child at the same hour every day "until the habit is formed." She advised occasional use of a soapstick suppository to start the movement in a constipated baby and to let the baby know "what is wanted." Although much "time and patience" would be required, West assured mothers that early bowel training would in the end be of "untold value to the child . . . throughout the whole of life."[62]

Like experts today, West believed that regular sleep was crucial for growing children. She advised women to put children to sleep in their own beds in their own rooms, if

61. *Infant Care* (1980), 38–39; *Infant Care* (1914), 49–50.
62. *Infant Care* (1914), 51.

possible, and to schedule naptime around the household chores. Once in bed, the infant was to be let alone and neither played with nor picked up even if he or she cried. Crying without cause was one of the "worst habits he can learn, . . . which takes all the strength of the mother to break." Admitting that it might "sound cruel" for a mother to ignore a crying infant, West maintained that allowing this habit to continue would ensure a "spoiled, fussy baby, and a household tyrant whose continual demands make a slave of the mother." In contrast, experts in the 1980 edition told mothers never to leave a crying infant alone. "Don't worry about 'spoiling' the baby," *Infant Care* reads today. "Giving the needed attention during the first year will help build the trust which will help him or her learn more 'grown up' behavior later on."[63]

Although the 1980 edition of *Infant Care* has a laissez-faire attitude toward thumbsucking, dependence on pacifiers, bedwetting, and masturbation, experts in the 1910s and 1920s singled these out as particularly common and difficult habits to break. However, West believed that harsh punishment would only draw attention to the habit because babies know "nothing of right and wrong." Instead, children should be diverted from bad habits, their energy guided into "wholesome and normal directions." According to West, most of the "naughtiness" of infancy could be traced to physical causes, and bad habits therefore were best controlled by physical means.[64] She recommended putting mittens on thumbsuckers or pinning their sleeves over their hands and tying the legs and arms of masturbators to their cribs or placing towels or pads between their thighs. Me-

63. *Infant Care* (1914), 60–61. *Infant Care* (1980), 18.
64. *Infant Care* (1914), 62–63.

chanical restraints had the added advantage that the mother did not have to constantly watch the child to make sure he or she was doing nothing wrong.

Despite her (to the modern reader) harsh advice, West conveyed a sympathy and respect for mothers to which women evidently responded. First, she showed an understanding of the financial constraints so many women faced. Although West's advice assumed a middle-class income and took for granted a "standard of life for the family high enough to permit a woman to conserve her strength for her family," she recognized that most readers would be unable to attain this ideal and occasionally offered cost-cutting suggestions. Second, West, a mother herself, was conscious of women's need for rest and to keep housework to a minimum. She encouraged mothers to get out of the house and allow some time for rest and recreation every day. She thought that the family, especially the husband, should protect the nursing mother from "*unnecessary* work and worry." Indeed, West's emphasis on schedules and regularity—more than the child-centered care and feeding on demand of the 1980s—kept the time women devoted to childrearing to a minimum. Finally, the pamphlets demonstrated a respect for and appreciation of the mother's intelligence and critical role in the care of both sick and well children. West considered motherhood to be a profession and acknowledged that the child's life depended on the "coolness and wisdom" of the mother when a doctor was not available.[65]

In the bulletins and in letters to their readers, Lathrop, West, and the rest of the Children's Bureau staff sympathized with the considerable difficulties mothers had follow-

65. *Prenatal Care* (1913), 6; *Infant Care* (1914), 34, 63.

ing their advice. They offered encouragement and concrete suggestions to worried mothers but admitted, in West's words, "how impossible they might seem to you and to me if I understood your situation more clearly."[66] Despite their inability to provide women with the money or diagnoses they really needed, the Children's Bureau staff referred women to their contacts in welfare agencies and state health departments and occasionally sent along gifts at their own expense. The Children's Bureau thus functioned more like distant relatives than like a government agency. And women responded with the same intimacy.

Every Mother a Working Mother

The Children's Bureau letters show a striking contrast between the composed middle-class mother portrayed in the pamphlets and real women, who experienced a range and depth of emotions. Although the bulletins instructed new mothers to remain calm and happy, actual mothers were often overwhelmed by their combined household and child-rearing responsibilities. "I have so much to do, I have no time to teach, only to scramble through some way," lamented a Texas mother of nine.[67]

66. Mary West to Mrs. N.W., Washington, Mar. 16, 1920, File 4-10-5, CB.
67. Mrs. M.T., Texas, to Children's Bureau, June 23, 1916, File 4-6-0-3, CB.

Their correspondence provides a rare insight into the
world of poor women who did not work outside the home.
Like the days of the women who wrote them, the letters are
packed with detail. They ask many questions at once,
showing that women had many things on their minds. Food
preparation, cleaning and other household chores, and
wage earning or farm responsibilities meant that most poor
(and even middle-class) women had little time to devote
exclusively to their children. Yet infants demanded a great
deal of time. A 1926 survey of the wives of young professionals in Washington, D.C., found that they spent five
hours and seventeen minutes each day on feeding, bathing,
and dressing the baby, and on laundering and mending infant clothes (not including time spent on other household
chores or playing with the baby).[68] These tasks must have
taken even longer for women who had limited resources.
Even women who tried to heed the instructions in the bulletins found that inadequate medical care, the unavailabil-
ity of nutritious food and pure milk, other work responsibilities, abusive husbands, and poor health, as well as their
economic circumstances, made the advice impossible to
follow. And the contrast between the ideal and the actual
conditions under which women raised their children must
have increased their stress, anxiety, and feelings of inade-
quacy, adding to the emotional work of motherhood.

Nursing ill children was a particularly difficult and demanding task. Although infant mortality and disease were
more frequent among poor families, even middle-class
mothers, such as Children's Bureau physician Mendenhall,

68. Laura Cowley Brossard, "A Study of the Time Spent in the Care
of Babies," *Journal of Home Economics* 18 (Mar. 1926): 123–127.

had children who died. Caring for sick family members took time away from chores and cut into the household budget, but worry and concern made the burden especially great. One woman, who had lost her only other child, wrote the Bureau in "sheer desperation" because fear that her new baby might die "haunts me day and night."[69]

The Children's Bureau correspondence documents the gap between the competent medical practice assumed in the bulletins and the care women actually received. Although the Bureau staff persistently advised women to consult physicians, mothers' letters document their horrible experiences with medical care. Women asked the Children's Bureau to warn other women, lest they too suffer "endless torture, . . . worry and pain" because of the ignorance or carelessness of physicians.[70] Their letters eloquently document women's frustration and anger at their lack of control over doctors, and they also caution us against romanticizing the days before medical care was widely available. The stress and physical danger endured by women who cared for sick children without medical assistance or who delivered their babies without skilled help drove them to seek medical aid.

Women's feeling of isolation, so clearly expressed in their letters, added to the emotional trials of motherhood—and increased their dependence on the Children's Bureau. Women in rural areas often lived far from family, friends, and medical aid. Forced to rely on themselves, they had

69. Mrs. H.S., Virginia, to Children's Bureau, Dec. 4, 1917, File 4-5-3-1-3, CB.
70. Mrs. A.E., Minnesota, to Children's Bureau, Aug. 10, 1932, File 4-5-7, CB.

only the Children's Bureau bulletins to turn to for advice. Their letters also reflect women's confusion over the conflicting advice of doctors (who did not always agree among themselves) and neighbors, and over persisting superstitions and traditions and the new ways. Young women complained about "old-fashioned" doctors and about neighbors who fed infants whiskey, sauerkraut, cake, and pickles. "It is hard to always know the right thing to do when older people say some such things as I have mentioned," wrote one woman, whose neighbor said that swallowing a prune seed was good for the baby.[71]

The letters also document women's courage, resourcefulness, and ingenuity. In adverse conditions, they struggled to protect their families from hardship, helped other women deliver their children, modified prescribed diets, ignored the advice of doctors when their children did not get well, and actively sought help in times of need. Women wrote to the Children's Bureau for medical care and money for their children as well as for scientific information and advice. Their requests pushed the Children's Bureau staff to address their concerns and, ultimately, to develop legislation that would protect their children.

In child-care publications, in newspaper articles, on the radio, in letters, and at health clinics, the Children's Bureau convinced mothers that they had friends in the government who cared about their problems and recognized their contribution to society. Their interest was deeply appreciated. One young woman, whose own mother was

71. Mrs. F.D., Quebec, to Anna Rude, Dec. 18, 1921, File 4-5-8-1, CB. Mrs. E.I., Iowa, to Children's Bureau, Mar. 24, 1920, File 4-4-3-3, CB.

dead, wrote staff doctor Rude that "words cannot express what I feel for you in my heart." A Missouri woman concurred: "You know we women can talk heart to heart more freely with each other than we can explain to any man."[72]

In the context of today's cynicism about government competence and caring, the story of the Children's Bureau—a government agency with close ties to mothers across the nation—seems all the more remarkable. In clubs, child-welfare campaigns, and letters to the Children's Bureau, women urged the government to recognize their contribution to society and to direct the nation's resources toward the health and welfare of women and children. Their efforts played a significant part in the development of the U.S. welfare system. Now social resources are once again being directed away from human concerns toward military development. The work women do to raise the nation's children is still unrecognized and uncompensated; reductions in welfare programs have increased infant mortality among the poor, and conservative opposition to birth control and abortion threatens women's right to choose when (and if) to have children. Understanding the lives and work of our grandmothers illuminates the circumstances we face today; their dreams can inspire us to continue their struggle.

72. Mrs. F.D., Quebec, to Anna Rude, Dec. 18, 1921, File 4-5-8-1, CB. Mrs. G.W., Missouri, to Mary West, May 29, 1918, File 4-4-3-3, CB.

Chapter One

Before the Baby Comes

Now I Am Pregnant, and I Get So Nervous and Worry So Terrible

In 1927 Dr. S. Josephine Baker, child-welfare activist and director of the New York City Bureau of Child Hygiene, termed the United States just about "the most unsafe country in the world for the pregnant woman." In 1930, the United States had the highest maternal mortality rate of twenty-five industrialized nations. Only tuberculosis was responsible for more deaths of American women in their childbearing years.[1] Even women who survived childbirth feared the toll it took on their health and on their families. Their letters depict the fear, anxiety, and depression that were part of pregnancy for many women; they also document the conflict many women felt between believing persisting superstitions and following scientific advice. The letters from Mrs. A.P. particularly moved Julia Lathrop and were a factor in the development of the Sheppard-Towner Maternity and Infancy Protection Act.

---

1. Quoted in Antler and Fox, "The Movement toward a Safe Maternity," 375.

Mrs. G.W., Iowa (March 30, 1916)
To the Children's Bureau Department:—

I am the mother of 2 healthy Boy's living, one little girl dead. When first child was born, I got a blue place on my right leg, as big as a dollar just above the knee, and [it is] getting worse every time a child was born. [I] have a blue place below the knee working down to the ankle, called Vari[c]ose veins. Dr's told me there is no remedy for it but an Elastic stocking which i wear, above and below the knee. It helps some for the swelling (knee begins to swell now to[o]), but the leg feels so hot, and when i stand up i must be so careful. [It] feels as if all the blood rushes to these places, and [will] burst out.

Now I am Pregnant again and get so nervous and worry about it so terrible that i will not be able to care for my family if something isn't done or cannot be done to it. Im very down hearted also about this. Before supper, i remembered this Department so I write, hoping to Recieve an ans. [I am] otherwise in good health, never sick nor a cold last winter. The last 2 or 3 months before child-Birth I must Urin[a]te so often, every 15 mint. Cannot hold Urine that long even. Sometimes water runs all the time for a little while. If i keep it up, i get pain. Otherwise have no pain. Babies are born in a hurry. [I] was sick only one hour of the last two Children.

My baby Boy is 16 months old now [&] is far from a healthy little fellow. He has quite some trouble cutting teeth, was quite sick of his eye-teeth, weighs 25 pds, eats every thing a child may eat of his age. [I] give him Nestle's Food and cow's milk. Do you think cows milk is good to drink during the hot Summer weather?

Will be very glad with any information or advise given to this letter.

*Grace Meigs responds that varicose veins and frequent uri-
nation are "fairly common" in pregnancy and urges Mrs. G.W.
not to worry about her condition, "though it must indeed be a
very uncomfortable one."*

Mrs. A.P., Wyoming (October 19, 1916)
Dear Miss Lathrop,
        I should very much like all the Publications on the
Care of my self, who am now pregnant, also the care of a
baby, both No. 1 and No. 2 [of the] series.
    I live sixty five miles from a Dr. and my other babies
(two) were very large at birth, one 12-lbs the other 10 1/2
lbs. I have been *very* badly torn each time, through the
rectum the last time. My youngest child is 7 1/2 (and
when I am delivered this time it will be past 8 1/2 yrs). I
am 37 years old and I am so worried and filled with perfect
horror at the prospects ahead. So many of my neighbors
die at giving birth to their children. I have a baby 11
months old in my keeping now whose mother died—when
I reached their cabin last Nov It was 22 below zero and I
had to ride 7 miles horse back. She was nearly dead when
I got there and died after giving birth to a 14 lb. boy. It
seems awfull to me to think of giving up all my work and
leaving my little ones, 2 of which are adopted—a girl 10
and this baby. Will you please send me all the information
for the care of my self before and after and at the time of
delivery. I am far from a Dr. and we have no means, only
what we get on this rented ranch. I also want all the
information on baby care especially right young new born
ones. If there is *a[n]ything* what I can do to escape being
torn again wont you let me know. I am just 4 months
along now but haven't quickened yet. I am very Resp.

Lathrop responds that she read Mrs. A. P.'s letter with "most earnest attention and sympathy. . . . It is not the only letter of that kind which the Bureau has received, —it makes very urgent the great question of protecting motherhood." She explains that the Bureau is trying to find a plan by which mothers in remote areas can secure the medical and nursing care "to which they are entitled." "It is an old need, but a new practical question, and it will not be solved until many people can be made to see that a way to provide the required care is possible in every part of our country. . . . Although I am no physician, I cannot but think . . . that you must have splendid natural vigor and powers of resistance to have emerged successfully from the birth of your other children, and I earnestly hope that things may be better next time. Certainly the world needs just such generous mothers as you are, and I am sure you are destined to go on helping your own and other people's children for a long lifetime." The Children's Bureau staff made a contribution to Mrs. A.P.'s layette out of their own pockets and sent a public health doctor to examine her. Other letters from Mrs. A.P. detail the experiences of other women in the area.

Mrs. A.P. (November 21, 1916)
My dear Miss Lathrop,

I had written you the night before Dr. H. came to our home. But I think she can tell you the contents of my letter much better than I can write it. I can not thank you enough for sending her out here. Not alone for the good she has done but because she is so good and dear. One can not help *loving* her, and wanting her to stay all the time. It has certainly been a wonderful two days for me.

I think she found me in fairly good condition. She will I am sure let you know just how everything is.

I am sure her coming has opened up chances for a great many things out here this country has needed. It seems strange that conditions can be met year after year as they have been out here that have been perfectly needless. It is only necessary to make the people realize that their conditions are not normal. And I am certa[i]nly glad if I can help in any way. Again thanking you for all your kindness, I am Sincerely.

Mrs. E.G., Indiana (June 18, 1918)
Dear Sir
        I saw in St Louis Weekly Globe Democrat Free book on Maternity. I am a wife of a soilder & will become a mother in about 8 months. My friend come out to See [me] with a baby Defarm[ed]; it[s] head like a snake. Can you tell wheather that would make my baby defarm[ed] by looking at It? I look at [it] about 10 Minutes. May was my first Month I didnt have my monthly so my time has come for June. Monday June 10 I taken sick in my stomach, try to thro[w] up But could [not]. My head hurt me & my side. I was sick Monday Eve then all day Wednesday & not since. So Please write; tell if that will defarm a baby & is there any thing I can take that will help it. I saw the baby Sat 15.
        Can you let your Husband have it after you are in that kind of shape & how long? When would [we] hofto stop doing It? Will I Ingure the baby in any way? Please write & tell & send me your book. Can you send me some pretty names for boys & girls that would be nice to name a baby?
        I always have my monthly on 29 or 30 of each month. When could you com[m]ence doing [it] after the child is

born. How long would you hofto wait? Please give full
information about such thing. I often hear they people
[are] not having baby. What do they do not to have them?
But I am crazy for Some Children & so is my Husband. I
remain.

    *Anna Rude assures Mrs. E.G. that she need not worry be-
cause a mother cannot mark her children. Although "it is very
hard to give set rules," she recommends total abstinence during the
latter months of pregnancy and suggests avoiding frequent sexual
intercourse "depending entirely upon the woman's discomfort."*

Mrs. H.R., Georgia (June 14, 1920)
Dear Madame

    I need advise. I am a farmers wife, do my household
duties and a regular field hand too. The mother of 9
children and in family way again. I am quar[re]lsome when
tired & fatigued.

    When I come in out of the field to prepare dinner my
Husband & all the children gets in the kitchen in my way.
I quarrel at them for bening in my way. I tell them I will
build them a fire if they are cold. I also threaten to move
the Stove out on the porch. What shall I do? My
Husband wont sympathise with me one bit but talks rough
to me. If I get tired & sick of my daily food & crave some
simple article, should I have it? I have [helped] make the
living for 20 years. Should I be [de]nied of a few simple
articles or money either? Does it make a Mother
unvirtuous for a man physician to wait on her during
confinement? Is it Safe for me to go through it Without
aid from any one? Please give me Some advise. There
isent any mid wives near us now. I am not friendless but
going to you for advise too keep down gossip. Yours.

Asking permission to publish Mrs. H.R.'s letter, Lathrop writes: "I have just read your letter of June 14 and I am deeply touched by it. I know you are a good woman and a devoted mother. . . . The Government of the United States through the Children's Bureau is trying to make this country easier for mothers and babies and I know your honest letter would help some men and women to understand why mothers ought to have better care."

Mrs. C.T., Tennessee (June 29, 1921)

Will you please send me any free booklets on the care of the expectant mothers and child? I am a farmers wife only thirty three years of age, the mother of seven children. This is the eighth pregnancy, and I am in real bad health and am quite unable to have proper medicine, diet or clothing.

My husband does not see any necessity of any extra care of my health now, and says it is only foolishness. So I am quite at a loss to know what to do. [I] have been in bed most of the time for 6 or 7 weeks without much care, as it takes quite all my little girl's (who is fifteen years old) time to do the housework and care for the smaller little one. Please send me any reading matter that might help me as I like to read. Your friend.

Florence McKay urges Mrs. C.T. to follow the suggestions regarding hygiene, diet, rest, exercise, and clothing contained in Prenatal Care. *"It is quite important for a mother during pregnancy to have especial care for her health. Farmers realize this in regard to their livestock and it is even more important to the mothers of children. . . . If attention is paid to such care during pregnancy much trouble is saved later on both for mother and baby."*

Mrs. C.T. (September 19, 1921)
Dear Miss Lathrop:

I wish to write you for a little advise, as I've read the article in "Holand's Mgzn" entitled "The dawn of Womans Power," and as I do not seem to get any strength and energy any more. I expect to become a mother in the early new year. Have not had any health this last several months. I've already a nice supply of booklets regarding motherhood, also a nice personal letter from the Dept that I ap[p]reciated very much indeed. The letter advised me to have the advice regularly of a Dr, tho that seems impossible for me to do. And also, I have not been able to procure the ne[ce]ssary clothing I need.

Am awfully nervous, and do not sleep well at night, and have a feeling of blues not at all pleasant. Will you please write me a letter and tell me please what will the Child Welfare and Maternity Bill that has passed in Congress do for us mothers and wives of farmers and working men? Will it be possible to get those nessasary things such as medicine, bed dressings, ect.? Please tell me. I thank you very much. We live near a small town where there is no hospital or nurses to be had, even [if] I'd be able to afford them, which I would not. I guess the Bill I've refer[r]ed to would not do any good outside larger towns, and expect this letter will sound foolish but please pardon and answer if you will. Respt yours.

Rude writes that "it is not unusual for an expectant mother to have times of feeling nervous and blue. If you are otherwise well, it is better not to pay too much attention to these feelings, but to try to do or read something cheerful to help you to overcome it." She describes a way to make inexpensive bed clothings and suggests that Mrs. C.T. seek a county or Red Cross nurse.

Mrs. M.A., Minnesota (October 19, 1921)
Dear Miss Lathrop:—
    Two or three years ago, I wrote you for some
pamphlets on "Care of the Baby" etc. I received them
O.K. and found them very useful. But after my last Babe
was two years old I gave away one or two of the pamphlets
to a relative who has since gone away.
    I'm to have another Babe in Jan. and I want very much
a pamphlet of some kind containing instructions on the
first things to do when the Baby arrives, the tying of naval
cord etc. We are 7 1/2 miles from a Dr. and tho that isn't
far in summer when cars are running, it's quite a distance
in winter, when roads may be bad and one must depend
on teams to get the Doctor when needed. I want to get
some practical directions so that a woman could do all the
necessary things if the Dr. was not in time. I thot you
would have the latest and best information and would
know just what to send me.
    My last Baby was born during the War and a flu
epidemic, and the two Doctors in our county were both
out, miles away when we wanted them. Neither one got
back to the office until our Babe was several hours old. I
am usually sick just a short time, 3 1/2 hours only with
our first boy. The Dr. arrived half an hour too late. The
second boy received the Dr's. attention as there was time,
but not the 3rd. Had no Dr. at all, but being a more experienced Mother and having my mother and a neighbor
Lady with me, we got along fine. I have 3 boys.
    I have been reading quite a bit about the work of the
Children's Bureau. Naturally, I am much interested in
the things being done for children. I consider them the
Nations most important asset, tho I sadly fear that some of

our politicians are blind to that fact. In the course of a few years the Babies of today will be directing affairs. How important that they should have some consideration. I wish to say that I appreciate your work very much, tho I am only one of the many common-place "Ma's." I wish you the best of success, and hope that most of us will be able to profit by the needful information obtained thru your office. I'm too far away to "shake hands" so I'll close by signing myself
Sincerely Your Friend.

Mrs. W.M., Milwaukee, Wisconsin (November 28, 1924)
Dear Madam:—

I have read in one of your library books that the Childrens Bureau sends out books or pamphlets called Prenatal Care & Infant Care to any mother to be, for the asking. I would be very grateful for these, for I have been told how easy you can mark a baby. It has really made me ill at times, & awfully nervous; even at a movie if an actor should put his hand on his face, I get a scared & sinking feeling around my heart. I worry & think, I only hope that wont or didnt mark the baby, simply because I was told a woman marked her baby by having had her hand on her face & [getting] a shock during a storm. Of course I try my very hardest to get over these feelings. I have no mother to ask these things & I'm afraid to ask other people, as I was scared enough already. So if you will send me these pamphlets I will certainly appreciate it very much. I only wish I had known it right away about 4 months ago. Thanking you, I am yours respectfully. P.S. Answer soon & keep this confidential.

Mrs. W.M. (February 10, 1925)
Dear Friend:—
    I am enclosing a stamp for an answer & am taking
the liberty to ask you for advice. You have helped me
before & told me I could write & ask your advice anytime.
    I am pregnant a little over 6 months. I had a longing for
strawberries for breakfast one day; I thought about them
before I got up, and while in the bathroom com[b]ing my
hair, I wiped out the corners of my eyes with my fingers. I
thought, well, it doesn't matter even if I haven't eaten any
strawberries yet. I asked a neighbor about it, & she told
me I sure must of marked the baby. Is this possible? She
told me if you have an appetite for anything & dont eat it,
& you put your hand on your face, or scratch your face,
that it will mark the baby sure. I'm just worried sick. Its
on my mind all the time. I wake up nights & think of
things to eat; it seems I just cant get that off my mind &
what can you do when you long for watermelon or mush
melon, or anything out of season? I cant get these things
now. Can that mark or harm the baby in any way? Oh
please tell me what to do. All these thoughts about
marking the baby when you dont eat what you think of, or
long for, just drive me frantic. I think of one thing, &
then I think of something else, but I try to overcome
these thoughts, & then I worry every time I wash or put
my hand to my face that I'm marking the baby because I
couldn't get or didn't eat what I longed for last. Does this
come from worry? I never worried about these things the
first few mo[n]ths, but her[e] of late I'm just sick from
worry. I couldn't tell this to anyone else but you, as I have
no mother, & no one else cares. I have kept it to myself,
but I just had to go to some one. & I'm sure you will help

me. I have your book on "Prenatal Care," but it doesn't say anything about longing for things to eat, so I just had to write and ask your advice. Thanking you very much. Please keep this confidentially. I am.

Replying to these two letters, Grace Abbott and Florence Kraker tell Mrs. W.M. that stories about women marking their unborn babies are founded on superstition and ignorance, and assure her that the best thing to do for a healthy baby is to follow the rules of hygiene contained in the bulletins.

Mrs. B.S., New York (September 28, 1926)
Gentlemen:

From the newspaper columns I learned that you send free information for the "Expectant Mother." My thankfullness will be unbound if you will please send one to me.

According to one doctor, [I] am allowed to eat everything "on earth" while another doctor tells me to eat nothing but milk, potatoes, butter; no eggs, vegetables or meats. I am in a great predicament as to which is which.

By nature [I] am jolly, fun-loving and healthy. (I mean I was.) By some trick of Fate or perhaps my own fault, I am now very very nervous, morbid, with no pleasant thought in my head except at great intervals. As I cannot afford good shows or good music, won't you please send me a list of good books? Hoping that I have not troubled you too much, I remain gratefully yours.

P.S. Am 4 1/2 months pregnant and I hope and pray to the Lord that I will "carry on" and through to a good finish. Please write "Personal" on the envelope.

Viola Russell Anderson writes, "As for your nervousness

and depression, we have to say that this is not an unusual condition in the pregnant woman. The remedy for it lies largely within the woman herself. She should try to overcome her fears and as far as possible keep herself surrounded with cheerful things. This means also that it is best for her not to discuss her condition with her friends and acquaintances who unintentionally often frighten her by telling her all of the sad things which have been known to happen. . . .

"We hope that you are going to see your doctor at least once a month, and that you are following carefully all directions which he gives you. The women who have proper care before the confinement and at the time of confinement are not likely to have great difficulty and usually produce fine healthy babies. Thus safeguarded, you may quiet your apprehensive fears."

Mrs. H.H., West Virginia (October 17, 1927)

Again I am asking information & your advice. I am a childless mother having lost my little one at the age of three weeks two years ago, & am pregnant again. My baby weighed 10 lbs. Overweight wasnt it? She was very greedy [and] never seemed to have enough to eat. I had no milk, so had to feed her [by hand]. My neighbors say if I didnt have any milk the first time that I will not have this time. Is this true? Please tell me if there is anything I can do for my self before baby comes? Some Drs or writers say to *lace & diet* while with child & the[re] will be no danger of over weight babies (is this *true?*) Any advice given will be closely followed. Thanking you for the information already given, & hoping I shall hear from you again soon. I remain yours truly.

Anderson writes that a mother can "almost always" nurse

her baby if she has had proper care during pregnancy. She sug-
gests Mrs. H.H. follow one of the diets she has sent and adds
that the average woman should not gain more than twenty
pounds. A physician should "help you decide" on diet and
weight.

Mrs. J.P., Cincinnati, Ohio (received November 17,
1927)
Dear Sir.
 Kindly send me books on Prenatal Care. I am a
broken-hearted mother, having lost my baby *10* months
ago, and am ready to go back in about 5 months. Don't
you think this is much to[o] soon to undergo such a strain?
I was *very very* happy with the coming of my other baby,
and then lost it, but with this baby I feel sad and blue. If
there is anything you can tell me, kindly answer.
Respectfully.
 Anderson suggests that Mrs. J.P. write to the Division of
Child Hygiene in Ohio. "Sometimes a sad and blue feeling
comes when a woman is pregnant, as one of the symptoms of
pregnancy, especially when she has had such grief as you have
had. When this happens it is just as necessary to try to keep your-
self cheerful as to have the proper food and rest. You must get out
of doors in the sunshine, see your friends, and not neglect to
have your usual amount of recreation. It may be an effort to go
out and do things, but the result in your improved spirits makes it
well worth while."

I Would Far
Rather Ask You Than
Mother

Women wrote to the Children's Bureau a variety of questions that they were afraid or ashamed to ask in person. Those who were ignorant or afraid of sex, who wanted children but were unable to have them, and even one who feared the effects of an abortion found that the Bureau offered a sympathetic (but safely anonymous) ear. These letters show the stress that resulted from women's isolation and ignorance about sex and reproduction.

Mrs. G.W., Missouri (May 29, 1918)
My Dear Mrs West:
      I wrote you about a year ago for two books which you promptly sent me and I found good advise in them. They were "Parental Care" and "Infant Care." They have proven themselves very valuable to me but I have a question before me now they do not answer, and I am writing to see if you will answer it personally. You know we women can talk heart to heart more freely with each other than we can explain to any man.
      I will state my case as briefly as I can. I have a baby boy who will be 11 months old June 13th. I got up when he was 10 days old and I did not flood very much, only it

lasted for such a long time, nearly six weeks; then after it
stopped for two weeks it came on me again and I was
unwell at irregular intervals for some time. Then when I
got regular I was unwell two months when I should have
been. Now I havent be[en] unwell since the baby was
seven months old, and, as I don't know whether I'm
pregnant again or not, I do not know whether I wean my
baby or not.

He has had indigestion more or less ever since he was
2 weeks old, and now he has a rash on his neck and back
& isn't growing as he should. He has five teeth. If you
would [advise] me what to do, I would certainly appreciate
it. Had I best wean my baby? I hate to do that so badly as
hot weather is here. Or had I better consult a physician
first? I haven't felt any signs of pregnancy yet. I am as well
and hardy of a morning as any other time of day. Please
ans. this if you can.

Mrs. G.B., Oregon (February 9, 1921)
Dear Sirs:—

Please send me you[r] information on the welfare of
mothers and children. I am a bride of two mo[n]ths and
know verry little on this subjuct. I would far reather ausk
you than mother.

How can you first tell when you are in the family way?
How many times may you interview with husband? My
mother and her family are subject to haveing twins; do
you think I will too?

I had a goiter; do you think my children would have
one too? Do you think it right if one knows how to stop a
childs birth to do so? I dont. I am not a verry strong girl

and am only 18 years old, do you think I should avoid
these things for a while? Please answer soon. Yours.
   Rude advises Mrs. G.B. that, "under normal conditions,"
intercourse occurs about twice a week but that during pregnancy
"the frequency rests with the wife. If it causes any discomfort, it
may be much less frequent. . . . It is not right to stop a preg-
nancy," Rude continues. "It is not only dangerous to the mother
herself, but also the taking of another life. I quite agree with you
in your opinion on the subject. You say in your letter that you are
not very strong, are you being as careful as you can about your
own personal hygiene? . . . It is particularly important to pay
attention to these things if you are preparing for pregnancy."

Mrs. W.O., Illinois (August 17, 1921)
Dear Madim:—
   I have heard when there is a Girl and boy twins, the
girls will not have children. I just learn't this. I am a twin,
wish you would tell me what you could and if a person
could doctor the truth. Thank you for the above
information. Yours truly.

Mrs. D.O., New Mexico (December 19, 1921)
   Please send me a medecine and an advice so I can
give birth to children. I was married 20 yrs ago, and I
have never give birth to children. I never have had a baby
nor a miscarriage in all my life and I feel sick always. I
want you to send me an advice [on how] to give birth at
time and tell me how I won't miscarriage. If I get pregnant
I am afraid to miscarriage because its a long time I am

married and never give birth to any children. Please ans as soon as you can. Yours truly.

Miss M.K., Illinois (February 22, 1922)

Not knowing where to obtain the information desired, I am writing to you in the hope that you will be able to furnish me with the information I am seeking. Not requiring a doctor for many years I do not like to approach a stranger for this information.

Sometime this spring I expect to be married. My honeymoon will be spent, if conditions permit, in touring Europe. My fiancee and myself are very anxious to have children, and it is because of this fact that I am seeking help from you.

I am an orphan, 35 years of age, weigh 106 lbs and am 5 ft 2 in. tall. My fiancee is two years my junior. As long as I can remember I have been in very good health. Practically no pain, or trouble, such as is experienced by many women, has bothered me during menstruation. For the last few years I have been working steadily at the strenuous job of managing about forty office clerks, so you see my general health must be pretty good. Occasionally in the evening for exercise I take long walks of several miles. This I seem to be able to do without any particular discomfort or apparent physical exertion. My appetite has always been splendid, and I sleep well.

However, I have been told by many would be friends that child bearing for a woman of my age is a very risky business. What do you think about it? Of course, I would not like to become pregnant on my honeymoon to Europe, but I do not want to delay the happy event at all after my return.

I have tried to diagnose my case for you that you might the more readily prescribe for me. Probably a system of exercise or diet would be advisable for me to adopt in order to more easily and safely perform the function of reproduction? Do you think I am underweight? Perhaps you can recommend some literature on the subject which I might read. Any information which you can give me toward helping me to become a happy prospective mother will be greatly appreciated. Sincerely yours.

P.S. Please send me copies of the pamphlets on "Prenatal Care" and "Infant Care."

Mrs. F.S., Cincinnati, Ohio (July 31, 1922)
Dear Madam:

I noticed on the "Woman's Page" of the "Post" a short time ago an article concerning child birth. I am a young married woman 20 years of age, and "my mother" died when I was 12 years old. I dont know much about these things, but perhaps you can help me. Home is so monotonous all day that I have gone back to my old position as a window trimmer and my husband is an Electrical Engineer. We both make good mon[e]y and can afford most anything we desire, but we are very thrifty.

I was married in June, and 3 months after my marriage I became pregnant and suffered from severe vomiting and dizziness. Nothing I ate or drank agreed with me. And neither myself or my husband knew what to do. We were living in a flat building at that time, and the lady across the hall told me of the sympathy she had for me and also told me of a doctor that could help me. And with my consent the doctor did so. I was nearly 3 months pregnant by now and the Doctor used a silver tube from which he

pumped air into the uterus. I felt allright until the next
day, then I became very weak and very dizzy again and was
sick in bed for 3 weeks before I was able to be up and
around again.

I have regretted the day I ever went to that doctor,
since I saw the little creature that I killed, my own flesh
and blood. It was just like a little doll and now I am afraid
I can never have any more children. My hubby and I are
just crazy to have a baby. But I am afraid I cannot, please
tell me if I can ever be a mother or not. Will be grateful
for any information you can give me. Please take this
letter of mine in your utmost interest. I will be willing to
pay for a charge if there are any at all for information
concerning my case. My only goal in life is to be a
mother. Yours respt.

Ethel Watters writes, "I am very sorry that you should have
so unfortunate an experience but nature is usually very kind and
she does not always punish by depriving women of children when
they have destroyed only one child. . . . It would be wise for you
to go to some good physician and have a careful examination
made."

Mrs. E.M., Indiana (January 22, 1925)
Childrens Bureau:

I read a peace in todays paper from you Explaining to
mothers the necessary growth of Childrens unto expectant
mothers, and while Reading, I begain to think. And a
mind come to me to write you a few words about myself
and see if you could tell me something that I could do that
would be a help to me. I am a strong woman and are 32
years of age and has always wanted children in my home

of my own, and hasn't any. I have taken all kinds of
medican but have failed to get the kind that would do me
any good. And I kindly ask that you advise me what I
should do that would be a help to me in that Respict.
Thanking you very kindly. Awaiting your earlyest reply.
Very trully yours.

Mrs. R.L., Idaho (November 5, 1926)
Gentlemen:
    My sister-in-law gave me the literature you sent her
to read. I expect to be sick in Dec or Jan and wanted to
write and ask you about sexual intercourse during the
period of gestation. I have been told this should be
avoided. I don't understand why and wanted to be sure.
Any advice would be greatly appreciated.
    I have been married for almost two years, and at
times I have no desire for sexual pleasures under any
circumstances, and if I do indulge in such, I feel more
pain than anything, as my sexual organs do not seem to
respond. While this is my condition a lot of the time now,
It was also very frequent before I became pregnant. Would
constipation have anything to do with this? I am very
constipated, and my bowels depend upon a laxative all the
time, which I have been taking all the time lately. I use
Rexall Orderlies. I have been in this condition ever since
I was a mere child. I am 20 years old now.
    Expecting to recieve your advice soon, I am.
    *Quoting from Dr. Robert Normandie's Standards of Pre-
natal Care, Anderson advises against intercourse during the
time the patient would have a period were she not pregnant. The
middle trimester, she says, is the most safe, but intercourse*

*should be avoided during the last two months because of the risk
of infection.*

Mrs. E.B., Mississippi (August 18, 1927)
Dear Mr. Stork

Have you any babies that you can spare? We won't
one. We live at ———. Will you please bring us one? We
won't a girl. Bring her and put her on the bed. If you
haven't any, please write me and tell me w[h]ere I can get
one.

*A copy of this letter was sent to the Mississippi Bureau of
Child Hygiene to be followed up by a public health nurse. The
Children's Bureau files contain no record of the result.*

Mrs. O.B., Missouri (February 23, 1932)
Dear Friend,—

So I am writing to get a few Information as an
expectant mother, as I am to be a mother of a child In
July. First, is how can a women tell that her [baby] is going
to be born? I am So Fraid I can't tell, and Won't be able
to get my doctor In time. *Ans.* And an other thing I
would like very much for you to explain is, I have heard
lots of them Say, When the baby is born, That the doctor
cuts on the women where the baby passes through. Is that
So? *Ans.*

As I am only 18, my first child to have, my husband
Says he doesn't want me to have any more. What Can
you do to avoid thems? People have told me that when a
child is born, the doctor can fix a women So She Can
never have any more childrens. Is that So? Now how can
they? *Ans.*

Now would you please ans my letter and questions I have ask[ed] you. For they would help me. I worry So much a bout it. Ans soon. Sincerely yours.

Blanche Haines suggests Mrs. O. B. write the state board of health for a public health nurse and advises her to find a good physician to care for her during confinement. She describes in some detail the signs of childbirth: discharge, labor pains, and sometimes "a gush of water." "You can ask your doctor whether he will make any cuts when the baby passes through. I think he will not do this unless it makes it easier for you. Sometimes it is easier to have the cuts than it is to have more pain. Don't worry about that, and don't worry about having more babies. Just get through this one first and you may not be so afraid to have another one. I think it would be a very bad plan to have anything done at the time of the birth of your baby to try to prevent any more coming. It would be very dangerous to do anything of that kind at that time.

"You know, a great many women have had children and more than one, and have lived through it and are very happy that they have their families. I think that will be the case with you."

Chapter Two

Raising the Baby

There Is Too Much
Foolishness Attached
to the Feeding
of Children

Many of the letters women wrote to the Children's Bureau concerned diet, both because gastrointestinal problems were a major cause of infant disease and mortality, and because cooking was one of the most important and demanding of household chores. These letters document the contrast between the diet recommended in the bulletins and the food available to most women. They show that although many women tried to follow the advice, others chose to ignore it, preferring to feed their children in traditional ways. Still others expressed bewilderment over the conflicting instructions of doctors, neighbors, and the bulletins. The Children's Bureau urged women to heed their doctors' advice and ignore the suggestions of friends, which, "though meant in the kindest spirit," had no "scientific value." [1]

Mrs. N.W., Texas (February 2, 1916) [2]
Dear Sir:—
    Please send me your book "Infant Care." I would appreciate very much if you could advise me in regard to my 28 months old baby boy. As we live in the extreme Southwest we do not always get fresh vegetables, with the exception of cabbage, onions and lettuce, nor do we always get fresh fruit. He is very sallow looking, tongue is always coated, sometimes constipated, altho I give him castor oil and castoria; these help temporarily. His ears are yellow looking, no blood seems to be in them. He looks to be anaemic but I really don't know what to feed him.
    I cannot always get a chicken when I need one for him and nothing in beef except round steak which isn't always fresh. The doctor here told me he'd outgrow his anaemia and coated tongue but I doubt it, as I never got over my anaemia and have a very weak stomach. If it is possible for you to send me a prescription for a good tonic to build him up and give him an appetite I would be very thankful to you for same. Thanking you in advance for any favors you may give. I am, very sincerely yours.

    1. Viola Russell Anderson to Mrs. C.S., New Jersey, Apr. 7, 1927, File 4-5-3-2, CB.
    2. Another letter from Mrs. N.W. is included later in this chapter.

Mrs. R.L., New York (May 10, 1919)
Dear Madam,

About a year ago your department was good enough to send me two books—"Prenatal Care" and "Infant Care"— both of which I have found to be very interesting and instructive.

On November 11th, 1918 I became the mother of twin babies, a boy and a girl. I feed the babies Horlick's Malted Milk and as they are now six months old I use quite a lot of it, a hospital size bottle lasting about five and one half days, and of course as they grow older they require more as the food is increased.

My druggist tells me there is a tax of fourteen cents on each bottle. As I use the malted milk as a food for the babies, the tax seems most unfair, for the children of to-day surely are the future of the nation. (Where all baby foods and in fact everything in the line of baby necessities are so high priced as it is, [it] seems almost unbelievable that the tax should be levied where it can be proven that the commodity is used only as a food for infants. That surely can not be classed as a luxury.)

In two weeks it costs us just nine dollars for food alone and I feel sure I am justified in asking if something can not be done to have baby food exempt from the tax. Perhaps yours is not the right department to address, but I feel sure if it is not you will be good enough to place it in the proper hands where it will at least receive consideration. If you can not do it will you be kind enough to advise me? Yours truly.

Dorothy Reed Mendenhall tells Mrs. R.L. that she will forward her letter to the proper department and advises her that cow's milk with gruel is less expensive and just as nutritious as Horlick's.

Mrs. E.I., Iowa (March 24, 1920)

Dear Sirs:—

Will you please send me the following pamphlets: West, Mrs. Max. Infant Care; West, Mrs. Max. Child Care; Mendenhall, Dr. D. R. Milk: The Indispensable Food for Children. Do you have any books or pamphlets concerning the digestibility of foods?

I have a little boy one year and nine months old, and some people insist on giving him cake, pie, cookies, doughnuts, etc. in spite of my objections. They have even said he could have pickles. Why should pickles be any more digestible because they are "well spiced?" Are not spices constipating? I was shocked beyond measure when after my baby swallowed a prune seed, a lady said, "It wont hurt him, is good for him, the rough surface will hold particles etc." Am I not right when I say that the stomach starts to work on any thing it receives, and if it is some indigestible thing that work is harmful to the child? I am trying to raise my baby to a strong healthy boy, but it is hard to always know the right thing to do when older people say some such things as I have mentioned.

Recently my husband asked, "how old must he be when he can have pickles," and I could not answer that, only I know he can't have them now. If you can send me any pamphlets, or tell me where I can get some that have to do with any of these questions I would be very grateful. Hoping I am not taking too much of your time with this letter. I am respectfully.

Letter sent to *Successful Farming* magazine and copy forwarded to the Children's Bureau (December 29, 1920).

Please publish the following regarding what to feed

children from three to ten years of age. Your issue of
December has made a statement with which I do not agree
at all.

I have five children; the eldest will be 13 years of age in
March, the youngest will be five in April. All of my
children are stout, healthy children. The eldest at thirteen
weighs 120 pounds, is well built and stout and is never
sick. The others in proportion to age are as heavy and
stout as he. I have not had a doctor for one of them for
over five years and never take medicine except for colds.

No stomach or constitutional medicine ever enters our
house. The way my children have been fed is as follows. At
the age of *three months* they were tied in a high chair and
fed well cooked potatoes, meat, bread and butter, all kinds
of fruit and vegetables in season. In fact they have eaten
good, wholesome farm food, just the same as I eat myself,
three times a day and usually a lunch just before going to
bed.

I was raised on a farm and have eaten good heavy food
all my life and at the age of 44 past, I can get out and do
as good a day's work as I ever could. In fact I can make
most of the young men up to 30 years of age ready for a
rest at night.

In my opinion there is too much foolishness attached to
the feeding of children in the present generation. I can
remember the food which children were given in the early
days of Kansas, which was plenty of cornbread, wheat
bread, potatoes, meat, seldom ever pie, cake or other
delicate pastry, and the young men of those days were
perfect in health and physique and stamina. On the present
system of raising children, in many instances the child is
ruined from too much attention to dieting and medicine.
My motto is, feed your growing children as you would your

young stock, to make size, strength, and a healthy vigorou[s] growth at an early age. I will conclude by saying that I was raised on a Kansas farm and am still farming in Colorado.

Mrs. L.R., Montana (November 4, 1923)
Dear Miss Abbott,

I am a mother with a baby boy who will be one year old November 30. Since he was born I have followed as carefully as possible the pamphlet "Infant Care," put out by the Government. I am enclosing the diet schedule I am using at present for my baby. It was given me by the head nurse of a baby clinic, where I took my baby periodically last summer.

The baby is in excellent health; and his diet seems to agree with him splendidly. The other day, however, I had him examined by a baby specialist here simply to assure myself that there was nothing wrong with him. This specialist said he thought the baby was too young to eat vegetables every day; that his diet should consist mainly of gruel and beef juice and broth, besides milk. He said that a young baby might develop some mucous trouble of the intestines from too much vegetable diet. I want to know whether he was right or not. When authorities and specialists disagree to such an extent, how can a mother have confidence in them? He also advised against the use of any sugar—not for my baby in particular, but for any baby.

When I am unable to secure fresh vegetables, is it all right to use canned peas and green beans? If you can advise me on these questions that are troubling me, I shall be very grateful. Yours respectfully.

Diet:

7 am.	cooked cereal (3–4 tbsp.) with milk, dry toast, zwieback or stale bread 8 oz. milk (boiled one minute)
9 am.	juice of 1 orange, prunes or fruit juices
12 am.	broth (4–6 oz.) or beef juice (2–3 oz.) baked or mashed potato or boiled rice (2–3 tbsp.) vegetable puree (2–3 tbsp.): carrots, spinach, peas, asparagus tips, string beans, squash, creamed onions, cauliflower, swiss chard toast boiled milk (4 oz.) Applesauce or baked apple
3 pm.	graham cracker or toast, or boiled milk (4 oz.)
5:30 pm.	cooked cereal (3–4 tbsp.) toast, zwieback, stale bread prune pulp & juice 8 oz. boiled milk

Mrs. C.A., Detroit, Michigan (March 2, 1926)
Gentlemen:
   Would you please send me your book called The Preschool Age—and also "Back Yards Playgrounds, Folder No. 2."
   I have a very important question I would like to ask—perhaps you do not take care of such individual matters,

but I am writing to inquire if you do. Here is my problem:
I have a fine baby boy, age 12 weeks, weight 12 pounds 6
oz. At first I had more than enough milk for him, but the
last 2 weeks I have not had enough, and had my doctor
give me a formula for to feed him part time—about 2 or 3
feedings a day. I do not understand why I cannot nurse
him as at first, for I think I drink enough fluids and I eat
quite a bit—but perhaps I do not eat the right foods. That
is what I want to know—*what to eat that is the best for my
baby*.

I do all my own housework—thought perhaps the
continuous work had something to do with not having
enough food for him. I am 26 years of age—this is my first
baby—and I do want to nurse him so badly. When I asked
my doctor again about it, he said, "Why don't you wean
him altogether?" But I have read so much about the
importance of breast feeding that I do not want to wean
him until all else fails. Anxiously awaiting your reply, I am
Very Truly.

*Viola Russell Anderson responds with a two-page letter on
breastfeeding. She emphasizes the importance of a well-balanced
diet, plenty of rest, the manual expression of the milk, and feeding by the clock. She suggests Mrs. C.A. give her baby a supplementary feeding after breastfeeding and lie down (but not sleep)
while she nurses her infant. "This takes [the mother] off her feet
for 20 minutes every three hours."*

Mrs. N.B., Michigan (July 20, 1926)
Dear Sir:

I read in one of your leaflet that there was no resin
why a Mother could not nurse her baby, if she had no bad

disease. There is not a thing [wrong] with me, only what I eat hurts me. I have a little Female weakness so it leaves me feeling weak. And we are poor farmers and have 4 children, so I have to over do. All so my milk leakes out. I have to give [the] baby cows milk alot of the time, and days I wash I have *no* milk. And when I have to give him the bottel all together, I can hardly get his bowels [to] move at all. And my milk is get[t]ing less all the time. So if I can't get help at once I must put him all together on the bottel, then what I am to do about his bowels I don't know. I have follow what you Dr's and my own Dr says as near as I can. So *please* tell me what to do.

Anderson sends Mrs. N.B. instructions on bottlefeeding and information on constipation. She also advises her to lie down when she nurses the baby. She continues, "We note with interest your statement concerning loss of your milk on the days which you wash. A mother can not give an adequate supply who is working too hard. Would it be possible for you to divide your washing over several days, doing a little at a time, so that you would not become so completely worn out?"

Mrs. J.B., South Dakota (March 4, 1927)
My dear Miss Abbott:

On pages 47–48 of the Bulletin "Infant Care," I find these statements: "If every mother realized how perilous the first months after birth are to her infant, and how great a protection breastfeeding is, few babies would be artificially fed, and as a result the number of infant deaths would be greatly lessened. Practically every mother with proper instruction as to the care of her own health can nurse her baby. . . ." Similar statements I find on every

hand, all implying that it is merely a matter of choice for a
healthy mother, living a hygienic existence.

I think no mother ever was more eager to nurse her
babies than I have been. It has always broken my heart to
wean them, and I have nursed them down to the last
drop—yet I have always "gone dry" in three or four
months. I have an abundance of milk at first, but in about
two months have to begin supplementing each feeding
with the bottle. Luckily I have always had excellent
results with artificial feeding; in fact the children have all
done better at once when put on the bottle. I have four
fine sturdy youngsters—the youngest, two months old, is
just beginning bottle feeding and like the others has made
splendid gains and shown marked improvement in the
character of the stools, since beginning supplementary
feeding.

I am a perfectly healthy woman, and have followed
most carefully every rule of hygiene laid down in the
Bulletin (& elsewhere). I always keep wonderfully well
when carrying a child and have such an easy time with
the birth—barely an hour and a half with the last baby
(8 lbs 5 oz) and really "nothing to it" at that.

Now *why* can I not nurse my babies? If I were alone in
my troubles I should not venture to write, but I have
known so *many* intelligent, healthy women, in precisely
the same predicament. We would give anything on earth
to be able to go on nursing till nine or ten months, if only
someone would tell us how.

When I said to my doctor, "Isn't there anything I can
do about it?" he replied, "Not *now*. You should have
begun 500 years ago." In other words, I'm "beef cattle"
and not "dairy cattle." We all know that this principle

holds true in the dairy, and that no amount of care and proper feeding, etc. can make milk records for some cows. If the same thing holds true with human beings, then the statements quoted at the beginning of this letter are not true. But if they are true, then there are some further factors involved which are not revealed in the bulletin. If there are such factors, can you tell me where I can learn about them? Anyone who can enable me to nurse my babies will win my eternal gratitude. Very sincerely yours.

Anderson tells Mrs. J.B. that "it has been our experience that practically every mother who had adequate care during her pregnancy and at the time of her confinement and who is a healthy woman can nurse her baby." She emphasizes the importance of adequate diet, emptying the breast at regular periods, and rest. "Rest is also interpreted to mean freedom from emotional stress and strain," she explains. "While we realize that the ordinary wear and tear of life means more or less stress, we also know that the mental habits of the mother have a great deal to do with this. In other words, the mother who has the worry habit and who sees the dark side of life has the wrong mental hygiene. We have known mothers who literally worried themselves out of their breast milk supply.

Mrs. C.S., New Jersey (April 6, 1927)
Dear Madam:—

Your very kind letter with phamplets received some time ago and I wish to thank you for same. Have had the baby to the doctors but really think my baby a puzzle and perhaps you can advise me better.

The baby is now 14 weeks old and the doctor has ordered 17 oz of Walker Gordon, 9 oz of water & 3 1/2

milk sugar, making 5 bottles of 5 1/4 oz every 4 hours, but
the baby always seems to be hungry before this. I try to
give her water in between this period, but [she] cries until
I give her the milk bottle. She certainly likes her bottle
and goes wild until she has it in her mouth and now
absolutely *refuses* to take the breast. Would you advise
giving the baby something to eat such as zwieback and
water or what would you suggest?

The baby is very active and does quite some crying and
fighting but only weighs 9 lbs 6 oz which certainly is not
enough for her age. [I] have the baby in the air all the
time (when not raining), but [she] still is quite pale.
Doctor says baby is OK but it does not seem so to me.
And as people advise me this & that, [I] don't know who
to listen to and am sure your advice would be more
correct.

Would appreciate your advice in this matter, as [I] am
very much worried that baby should get on better than she
is, as I give her all my attention. Thanking you very much
for any help you can give me. Beg to remain yours very
truly.

*Anderson responds that the formula is a "perfectly good
one." "We can only advise you to heed the suggestions of your
doctor and have absolute confidence in him," she continues,
"paying no attention to the suggestions of well meaning friends
whose advice, though meant in the kindest spirit, undoubtedly
can have no scientific value. . . . We appreciate that raising the
first baby is not the easiest matter in the world, but we think that
you should not worry too much. If you will give your physician
your entire confidence and feel that a great deal of the responsibility for raising the baby is in his hands, we hope that perhaps
you will feel less worried about the outcome."*

Miss G.M., Pennsylvania (March 22, 1928)
Dear Sir:
     Will you please send me the following booklets.
Please send me The Infants Care and The Mothers Care
or Parental Care booklets as I understand you will send
them free. My mother was just taken to the hospital for
appendicitis. And left me to take care of my 3 months old
sister who was nursing. I am starting her on cows milk and
milk of Magnesia 1 teas., 1/2 cows milk 1/2 water. Am I
feeding her enough according to her age? She seems
satisfied and sleeps well at night.
     Will you please send the books as soon as possible as I
am only 15 yr old and don't know much about a baby.
     Anderson sends Miss G.M. a copy of Infant Care *and
advises her not to feed the baby milk of magnesia.*

I Shall Be Glad
to Learn How to Cure
This Habit

The following letters illustrate the amount of time and
effort some women spent trying to get rid of their children's
"bad" habits. According to *Infant Care* author Mary West,
bad habits such as crying, thumbsucking, and masturbation
would lead to physical deformity and to a spoiled and weak
character. If allowed to continue, they would render the
child a tyrant and the mother (like Mrs. J.S.) a slave. West
warned parents not to punish infants with bad habits. Instead, she advised diverting the child's attention away from

himself or herself. She also recommended physical restraint, in part because it did not require mothers to constantly watch the children. Although the Children's Bureau staff sympathized with the mothers of babies with bad habits, they stressed the danger of allowing these habits to continue.

Mrs. F.H., Nebraska (July 5, 1915)
My dear Mrs. West:—
I rec'd your letter returning my manuscript "Tickling the Baby." I am so glad that you do not approve of this awful habit, and am glad there are two such sensible women at the head of the Dep't. as you and Miss Lathrop. If I had the ability to lecture I certainly would on this subject. It seems to be a common thing for people to tickle babies around their sexual parts, these organs are sacred and should not be harmed. If a child grows up a degenerate whose fault is it? Can you tell me why there is not a law against this?
I thank you very much for sending me the pamphlet on "Infant Care." It is simply fine: one of them should be in every home where there is a baby. It seems to me if a baby were taken care of according to your instructions in "Infant Care" it would surely be a normal child. Very respectfully.

Mrs. J.S., Washington, D.C. (January 10, 1920)
To the Chief of the Children's Bureau:
I am writing you for advice. I am a young mother, my baby will be thirteen months old the tenth of this month. He is not weaned yet, he eats from the breast all day and

part of the night. This pulls me down & makes me look
worn & be tired. I cannot get out of his sight a minute, if
he is not crying.

There is no real cause for crying as he is a health child.
Has not been sick & under the doctors since birth. I
cannot even get out a couple of hours for the pictures.

He has a crib of his own to sleep in but he will not sleep
in it. There is no one else at home with me except my
husband and he is willing to mind the baby while I get out
for a couple of hours, but he cries after me so that I am
afraid to leave home. Not even to the corner to mail a
letter.

I would like to know is it now too late to train him not
to cry after me. He has all kinds of toys & yet nothing
quiets him but me. Please send me some advice as to how
I can wean him & to stop him from clinging to me so. My
husband tells me to feed him good & let him cry himself
to sleep but this seems very cruel. Please make this letter
strictly private, as I am classed a very foolish mother.

*Anna Rude responds that a baby should be weaned by thir-
teen months and not fed oftener than four times each day. "It is
very important that your baby sleep alone and since he has not
been trained to do this from birth, you may have some difficulty
in teaching him to do so. If you know that the baby is comfortable regarding his clothing, and that he has been given sufficient
food, it is then wise to put him into his crib and let him cry it out.
In time he will acquire the habit of going to sleep alone.*

*"It is never too late to begin training and disciplining a child,
and I know from your letter that you realize that you will find it
more difficult than if you had begun earlier. I think the enclosed
dodgers offer the information which you will find most helpful in
weaning your baby, but if you find that you are not successful*

after a couple of weeks, I should be glad to talk with you if you care to come in."

Mrs. W.P., Ohio (January 26, 1922)
Dear Madame:
    I write to you to inquire whether you can suggest a means of dealing with an eleven months old baby who seems to consciously and persistently cross one of his eyes. He began doing this trick at ten months. We have hesitated to punish him because we supposed he was too young to understand. On the other hand, we fear he will do some permanent injury to his eyes. He is a perfectly strong healthy normal baby in other respects. Respectfully yours.
    Rude writes, "I quite agree with you that it would not do any good to punish an eleven months old baby for the condition which you describe. Many young babies appear to have a slight squint until the eye muscles are well developed. The only suggestion that I could offer you is that when the baby apparently does this 'trick' you should try to attract his attention to something at a distance and in this way prevent its becoming a habit. If the condition continues it might be advisable after one year of age to have the child examined by a specialist."

Mrs. R.C., New Jersey (April 4, 1923)
Miss Lathrop:—
    I am writing to you to see if you can help me, in a serious problem or what seems like one to me.
    I have four children. The eldest is six in June and the youngest is sixteen months. So you see they are very close together and I can't spare any big time on any one of them.

The Baby causes me much worry and keeps me continually on edge when she is out of my sight. She has, what you call in one of your books by Mrs. West, masturbation. Or at least that is what I should say it is. She does not undertake to put her hands in her diapers [and] never puts them on herself when she is bare. But when she sits up she works herself backwards and forwards.

The first I noticed it was early in the winter & I thought perhaps it was folding the diaper three cornered that made too much between the legs.[3] So I tried folding it square and keeping her washed clean. But it does no good. She does it most when she is tired or not well and lately every time I look at her she is at it. The only way I can get her to stop is to take her attention some way, and I haven't time to be always on hand to watch her. When she is not where I can see her I keep running to see if she is all right.

And I can't hold up much longer under the strain and worry of it. Having my children so close I am naturely not as strong as I might be otherwise and my nerves are in a bad way.

So if you could help me it would certainly be a big load off my mind. She seems to have a sort of discharge when she is the worst and is inclined to be constipated all of the time. She seems to be very bright mentally and is beginning to talk & sings too. She can not walk yet & I have thought perhaps that was the reason of it. Her legs tremble so when she stands up.

I can't bear to see her grow up that way, and if I

---

3. The ordinary diaper was cumbersome. Made of a square of material between one-half and three-fourths of a yard wide, it was folded twice to make four thicknesses of material. *Infant Care* (1914), 17–18.

thought she would I would rather she would die now. I
remember when I was a girl at school. Two different girls I
knew who used to ride their seats and I couldn't stand it to
think of my daughter acting the way they used to look to
me. So please advise me what to do and I will surely be
grateful for the favor. Respectfully yours.

*Ella Oppenheimer writes, "I realize how concerned you are
about the habit your youngest child has developed," and suggests
that Mrs. R.C. make sure the child is physically strong, not constipated, gets plenty of rest, and sees a physician for any discharge. She recommends surrounding the baby "with a few
simple playthings" when she is alone in order to divert her attention from herself. "Do not be too concerned about this [habit],"
Oppenheimer concludes. "She is very likely to outgrow it if she is
properly attended to at this early age."*

Mrs. O.G., California (December 19, 1923). Letter sent
originally to the Bureau of Home Economics in the
Department of Agriculture and then forwarded to the
Children's Bureau.

Though it is not in your line, can you tell me of some
one who can tell me of what to fix up to amuse the child
between two and three. I have one, whom I love more
than life itself, but it is a fact that I have not had a
minute's peace since he was born. He is healthy, but
alone, and extremely active, so much so that I do not see
how I am going to live until he gets old enough to go to
school or kindergarten, or someplace where he can have
something to do, and someone to do it with.

*Ethel Watters sends bulletins and a reading list to Mrs.
O.G. "It is not necessary that a child should have someone to*

amuse him all of the time. He should be put in a safe place to
play and given a chance to amuse himself."

Mrs. N.F., New Mexico (February 28, 1924)
Dear Sir:

I am writing to find out if you can let me know how
to break my 3 months old baby from sucking her thumbs
and fingers. I have keep her hands pin[n]ed down but as
soon as I unpin them she sucks them and she should have
the use of her arms. I put mit[t]ens on her and she even
sucks them. Please let me hear from you. Oblige.

Florence Kraker replies that "it requires some time and a
great deal of patience on the part of the mother whose baby has
acquired this habit." She suggests that Mrs. N.F. put small
splints of wood on the child's arms or pin elastic between the
child's sleeves and the bed so that she can move her arms but not
quite reach her mouth.

Mrs. J.L., Chicago, Illinois (November 7, 1925)
Dear Madam:

It is my understanding that you will answer questions
concerning our problems with children. I will be very
greatful to you if you will answer several of mine.

I have two daughters who[se] respective ages are two
years and six months, four years and ten months. Both of
them had the thumb-sucking habit. The eldest I broke of
this habit before she was a year old. Her sister is more
persistent and tho' I have tried every means I could
discover she still sucks her thumb. I first tried making

mittens for her of cotton cloth, then I put her in a
sleeping bag made of heavy outing flannel, next I covered
her thumbs with adhesive tape, and after that I tried two
different very bitter solutions, painting the thumbs and
then soaking the adhesive tape with them—none of these
were effective. About a month and a half ago I got a pair
of aluminum mittens and always have her wear them at
nite and when she takes her daily nap. Of course she
cannot suck her thumb when she has these mitts on but as
soon as I take them off she sucks it harder than ever.
Before I got the mittens she did not suck her thumb much
during the daytime. I do not feel that it is rite to have her
wear the mittens during the day as she would have not use
of her hands. I have tried having her wear them part of
the time during the day. She cries the whole time they are
on her in the daytime and sucks her thumb as soon as they
are taken off. I shall be very glad to learn how to cure this
habit.

My eldest daughter has a good disposition but she is
phlegmatic. I have a tendency to try to hurry her instead
of letting her take so much time to do everything she
does. Should I do this or should I just let her develop
naturally?

Should one never delude a child at all—even to the
extent of telling her there is a Santa Clause?

Do you think it wise to try to follow Ellen Key's
philosophy in having young children? I am now reading
her book "Century of the Child."

I should like to have Publication 143 and to know of
other literature on the subject of child training. Thanking
you kindly for your help with these problems of mine.
Very truly yours.

   *June Hull recommends improvising cuffs from cardboard,
pinning them to the child's sleeves so that they extend a little*

above the elbow, "thus preventing the flexing of the arm. This leaves the child's hands free for use in play, and she will only be prevented from bringing her hands to her mouth. These cuffs can be worn continuously except at meal time." Hull tells Mrs. J.L. that she is not acquainted with Ellen Key and that mothers have to decide for themselves how to present Christmas to their children. She suggests that Mrs. J.L. see a physician to determine why her child is slow.

Mrs. D.F., Newark, New Jersey (received May 11, 1927)
Dear Mrs. West,

I have one of your booklets on Infant Care published by the United States Department of Labor Series No. 2, and I am taking this liberty to ask you a personal question concerning my baby.

My baby girl for the past three or four months has gotten into the habit of crossing her legs and rocking to and fro and sort of bearing down at the same time, and some how or other I can't seem to make her stop. I have taken her to two baby specialists and they call it "Masturbation," and suggested putting a stick (or knee crutch) between her legs, but somehow or other it seems to do no good. I have even gone so far as to tie her legs to her crib, and also to her high chair when she is sitting, but she seems to be able to rock and breathe heavy just the same.

I am at my wits end, and feel that I cannot endure watching her any longer, as it is a most disgusting thing and is making a nervous wreck of me.

Now my dear Mrs. West if you could please offer some suggestion as to what other way I could stop her, or perhaps some doctor that you might know that specializes in such cases, I would appreciate same very much, and

certainly would never forget your kindness in this matter.
Thanking you in advance for your promptness in
answering or anything that you may do for me. I remain,
yours truly.

P.S. My baby is not quite eleven months old. Am
enclosing a self addressed envelope.

Anderson encloses Dr. Douglas Thom's bulletin on Child
Management. *"We would emphasize the point Dr. Thom
makes . . . concerning your own frame of mind," she writes.
"Masturbation in the child is an entirely different matter from
the same practice in an adult, and it is not just to the baby to
judge her from an adult standard. Because you are judging her
from this adult standard, you are making yourself unduly dis-
tressed. Masturbation in a baby should be thought of no more
seriously than thumb sucking, unless there is a definite physical
cause. . . .*

*"We know that this habit is a difficult thing for the mother to
resign herself to, but if you will realize that many babies go
through such a phase and that the matter means very little in the
infant, you will be able, we hope, to bring yourself to the frame
of mind when you can regard it impersonally. The danger to the
child . . . is in making the child self-conscious and in calling her
attention to the habit in such a way that she becomes so im-
pressed with it that she will not give it up. If you will offer her a
toy to distract her attention when there is a tendency to practice
the habit you may find that this will help."*

Mrs. W.G., Texas (August 27, 1927)
Gentlemen:

Some time ago I sent for your books on Care of the
Baby, Child Training and etc. I would like to get some
additional advice if possible. My baby is now 18 months of
age, has a good appetite, eats regularly, is in good health,

except for the fact that he is cutting his stomache and eye teeth, but he fights sleep; that is, his regular naps. When he does fall asleep, and especially at night, he crawls all around and often sits up in his sleep with the result that he is generally tired and sleepy shortly after waking.

When he was younger, he kicked and squirmed so that we pinned him down in order to keep him covered. At first just pinning the covers held him secure. Later we pinned the sleeves of his nightgown in order to keep him from crawling out of the covers and also the legs as he would kick his feet in the air and hold them in that position until they were stiff and cramped.

I do not know whether his restlessness is the result of having been pinned before or not but certainly would appreciate if you could give me any advice which would help him to sleep more quietly. Thanking you, I am, very truly yours.

Anderson replies that an eighteen-month-old baby no longer needs a long afternoon nap and suggests that overstimulation in the evening is a common cause of disturbed sleep. Once the child is put in bed in the evening, she adds, he should be left alone. She suggests that it is not wise to restrain a child of his age too much; little sleeping suits will cover him up even if he kicks off the covers. "Children vary in their sleep habits as do grown people," Anderson ends her letter. "Some of them are restless even though they are put quietly to bed, have not played too hard during the day, and are at peace with themselves and with the world."

Mrs. J.T., Wisconsin (September 8, 1927)
Attention Miss Grace Abbott

Please send a copy of the care of children Number eight (revised). At the same time could you give specific advice concerning a six month old baby boy weighting twenty eight pounds [and] perfectly healthy except that he cries three or four times during the night and has to be picked up and walked with.

There is no question but what he is spoiled, but he has such a lusty cry that my husband and I are afraid to let him cry long for fear he will rupture himself. We would be perfectly willing to allow him to cry all night if we were only sure that it would do no harm.

Have you ever heard of a baby harmed thru crying? Awaiting what ever information you may have I am Very Truly Yours.

A Dirty Child at Three Months Is a Mother's Disgrace

Today babies are not normally toilet trained until they are about two years old, but in the 1910s and 1920s mothers were supposed to begin bowel training at two months. Dirty diapers were a serious health hazard as well as a lot of laundry. Although these letters are evidence that some women began bowel training when the baby was a few months old, few mothers were as successful as Mrs. E.R. Even the "experts," such as Anna G. Noyes, who recorded her infant son's development in *How I Kept My Baby Well*, recognized that dry diapers were an ideal that did not often correspond with reality.[4] Although Noyes began toilet training her son

4. Anna G. Noyes, *How I Kept My Baby Well* (Baltimore: Warwick and York, 1913).

at two months, she did not worry when he did not have his first dry day until he was two years old. That the Children's Bureau received few letters on this topic suggests that even though women began toilet training at two or three months, they did not expect to have clean diapers.

Mrs. E.R., California (May 16, 1918)
Dear Madam,
    In reading your valuable pamphlet on "Infant Care"—on the heading "Diapers"—I observe that you take no notice of the fact (which may be unknown to you) that children may be made clean, and dispense with "Diapers" at an extremely early age. I am the mother of three children, a boy and two girls. My monthly nurse, a very experienced and clever woman before she left after being with me two months, showed me that by holding out babies of a month old, and making some suitable noise, they will do what is necessary immediately. And for bowel motions by placing them on the chamber, & making a grunting, indicating the action required, they will readily respond. The baby gets to know what is meant immediately.
    A well known book, Pye Chavane's "Advice to Mothers on the Care of their Children" by a distinguished English physician mentions the same fact and concludes his remarks by the words "A dirty child at *three* months old is a mothers' disgrace.". . . I trust you will not misconstrue my writing to you but I feel that if you could contribute to the disuse of diapers—dangerous, as you point out, in many cases—by this simple expedient you would be doing an important service to the mothers of young America.

My three children were perfectly clean at 3 months and
I never used diapers after three months. Begging that you
excuse the freedom I am taking, I am, dear Madame, yrs.
faithfully.

West replies that she is currently revising Infant Care *and
is "indebted" to Mrs. E.R. for her suggestions. "However, if
you will be good enough to look on pages 50 and 51 of* Infant
Care, *you will see that I have not ignored the need of training the
baby to the early use of the chamber."*

Mrs. R.B., Pennsylvania (November 9, 1924)
Dear Madam:
    I am following the advice of your Bureau Publication
No. 8—"Infant Care," on p. 42–43, "Training the
bowels." I started my baby at 2 months, sitting on the
chamber in my lap. She is now 3 months old. Her
movement does not yet come without the soap stick. I
know I should not continue its use so long. Can you
advise me further? Before I started the chamber, her one
daily movement came at 5 or 6 p.m. I give her the
chamber before her bath, at 9:30 a.m. Was it wrong to try
to change her hour so radically, and could that be the
cause of the difficulty? I have always been constipated but
by the use of Squibbs I have been very regular since she
was just about a month old. She is a breast-fed baby, with
one bottle a day.
    The problem is puzzling me considerably. I shall be very
grateful if you can tell me how to proceed. I shall hope for
an early reply. Thank you. Resp'y.
    *Hull writes that it usually takes only a few weeks to toi-
let train a baby using the method in* Infant Care. *She tells
Mrs. R.B. to try feeding her child orange juice, or possibly milk*

of magnesia, but warns her not to use a soap suppository any longer.

Mrs. F.S., Massachusetts (December 12, 1925)
Dear sir:
    Please send me the third bulletin on Child Care: The Preschool Age. Can you tell me how I can get my 2 1/2 yr old girl to make her bowel movements when on toilet? She soils her clothes every day. I have tried punishing by slapping and putting to bed with no results. I can't make her stay on; she waits till she gets off and soils her clothing. I have kept her on her chamber chair for as long as an hour, then have her get off, and inside of five minutes, soil herself. She is good about telling to empty bladder. Respectfully.
    Anderson suggests that the position of the child on the seat might be a factor in the ease with which she passes her stool. In addition, "a little friendly encouragement, possibly a reward for good behavior, is sometimes helpful. Little children do not always understand definitely just why they are punished."

Mrs. L.S., Ohio (January 30, 1928)
My dear Mrs. West;
    Have received a great deal of help from your pamphlet, "Infant Care." Thot you might be interested in a new method for teaching babies to have a regular bowel movement. This method I find more practical than the one suggested in your booklet.
    We have one of the baskets for babies that are so popular now days. During the night it is used for a bed but in the day time it serves as a toilet. For the latter purpose,

a section of newspaper is folded in half and laid in one half of the basket. The paper so folded is a little wider than the basket so the edges turn up as it is fitted into the basket. I pull the paper down a couple of inches so that the paper will be turned up at the foot as well as at the sides. The basket is then tilted about two inches by putting a block of wood under the end that does not have the newspaper. The diaper is taken off of the baby and she is laid in the basket so that the buttocks rests upon the lower end where the paper is. This is done after the first feeding in the morning.

My experience was that after using a soap stick a few mornings the baby learned the purpose of the paper. She seems unconcerned when put in the basket, but by the end of 15 minutes she usually has had a bowel movement. The baby often wets at the same time but the fluid runs down toward the foot of the basket. The paper is taken out, whatever can be is shaken into the toilet. Then the paper is burned.

I like this method for it takes so little of my time. I can be dressing my self or one of the younger children while I am watching the baby. When I tried the method you suggest of holding the baby she seemed to be distracted by the fact she was being held (she expected to be played with). It is an advantage to be able to do this the very first thing in the morning, for often the baby will not wait until bath time. The mother then has to stop during the breakfast time to change a soiled diaper. Have read that a baby will not wet itself so often if it can be made to urinate voluntarily part of the time. So I put the baby on the paper in the basket after each feeding. She will usually urinate in a few moments. However she often wets herself before I can get her into the basket. Yours most sincerely.

I Worry
Myself Nearly to Death
with Him

Many of the letters directed to the Children's Bureau concerned disease. In the letters below, women express their
distress and terror about sick children. They describe their
infants' ailments, many of which, such as colic, diarrhea,
constipation, and malnutrition, were related to digestion.
Ill children often had unhealthy mothers, but these women
could be resourceful and strong when they had to care for
sick children. Women asked the Bureau for assistance when
doctors were unavailable or when their advice did not seem
to help, but in every case the Children's Bureau urged them
to follow their physicians' instructions.

Mrs. E.C., Kentucky (September 23, 1915)
Dear Sir,
	I have re[a]d [your] helpful hints on caring for an
Infent Baby, but none suited my baby['s] case. I have a
Baby Boy [who] came the 4th day of aug. He has the three
months colic. I wor[r]y my self nearly to death with him.
The dr gave me colic tablets for it. He gave me some.
medocine to digest his milk. He is a breast baby. I am
heltie and hartie ever[y] way. He weighed 9 1/2 when he
come, now he weighs 12 1/2. He is fat and hartie. I have
fed him asifrettive & whiskey and calimel, tea, caster oil
& Charles H. Flitcher's castoria. He cries as soon as these

are out of him. I rec[k]on I warm a Sash, [w]rap it in a
flannel [rag] also. These all help him when he has it but
soon have to repeat it again. I want to [k]no[w] if you can
give me a remedy to cure it. I onely let him nurse ever[y]
2 hrs. His hands and feet is always cold when he has the
colic.

I have two more children, the oldest is a boy 10 years
old [the] 26 of the month. The girl will be 3 the 24th of
next march. There father is a heltie and hartie man. The
oldest boy was the same way this baby is. I just treated
him like I am treating this baby. The girl never cried
much, but the boys pays up for it. Everbody says there
ain't any cure for 3 mont[h]s colic, and I feel like
somebody has found a remedy by this time.

I eat all Vegetables but cabbage, sweet potato, onion. I
don't drink any thing but tea watter. The baby is also
constipated in his bow[e]ls. I saw in the journal a remiday
of orange juse for a baby 6 mon old, but I did not [k]no[w]
weather to try it on him or not. I saw this in the railway
Carman Journal. My husbay is a rail road man and he
takes this Journal. I would like to here from you at
once. . . . Answer at once please.

Mrs. N.W., Texas (February 18, 1916)[5]
Dear Madam:—

Altho I haven't heard from you regarding my boy
who is past two years old, I am anxiously awaiting your
reply to my letter and take the liberty of writing you again
in regard to his eyes.

Last March he was bitten in the forehead by a dog,

5. Another letter from Mrs. N.W. is reproduced earlier in this
chapter.

making a very deep hole directly over his right eye. The
dog's head was sent to the Pasteur Institute, Austin, and
they wired back the dog had no rabies. It had become
intensely hot in June when I noticed a small knot in his
left eye. I consulted an eye doctor here who prescribed
several kinds of eye drops and pastes but his eyes grew
worse, both became inflamed, and a film form[ed] around
the iris of both eyes.

After paying the doctor $12 for services which made
the eyes worse, I began treating them myself. I purchased
1 dozen small towels, boiled them thoroughly and used
them for his eyes exclusively, never using the towel more
than once. Used boric acid in eyes, but when this didn't
relieve inflammation, [I] tried hot applications and baking
soda in water instead of boric acid, which relieved them
somewhat.

When cold weather came, I noticed an improvement
and finally the inflammation disappeared. One day last
week, I noticed a small film again on the iris of his left eye
and up to the present time both eyes are again inflamed
and the film has spread around the iris of both eyes,
making his eyes look weak.

He always had clear, bright, pretty brown eyes with
long thick lashes. Now the lashes are falling out, and he
always rubs his eyes. The eyelids and around the lashes
look to be in a healthy condition, no redness whatever. A
good many Mexicans live here and the doctor thought his
eyes may have become infected from them. Or do you
think it has something to do with the dog bite?

Any advice you can give me will be so appreciated.
There is no other doctor here who can advise me and I
feel so helpless and like a prisoner who can't escape from
this hole.

Please send me the book "Prenatal Care." Last June I

gave birth to an 8 mos. baby girl who died 16 hrs. later. I
became very weak, [with] pains in both sides continually.
In Dec. I determined to undergo an operation. The
surgeon said I had [the] beginning of appendix trouble
(I had frequent dull pains around the navel), [and]
retroversion of the womb. He'd scrape [the] womb, sew up
laceration (was torn when my boy came two years ago and
never sewed), and heal ulceration of womb, and he might
have to cut a little off of an ovary. I had dreadful cramps. I
was treated for bowel trouble, and it wasn't until my baby
came prematurely that I found out it was my womb
cramping and the doctors didn't know what was the
matter with me. They gave me hypodermics which made
me sicker than ever but didn't relieve my cramps. So I am
begging you to help my boy and myself, if in your power. I
don't want to lose this baby, which, God willing, I expect
in August. I am very constipated; pills don't help me
much, except an enema. [I] have a heavy bearing down
feeling, vomit a great deal, and every now and then pains
at mouth of womb, slight pains in right side occasionally.
I had my last period on Nov. 21st.

Anxiously awaiting your letter, and again thanking you
for any advice you can give me. I beg to remain, very
sincerely yours.

P.S. I forgot to state that in the last two weeks I have
been cramping again. My just beginning to cramp again
reminded me.

Meigs writes, "We should like very much to be of help to
you, but as you must realize it is almost impossible for anyone to
give you information which would be of help to you without
seeing and examining both you and your child. Any medical advice which is of any value must be based on a thorough and scientific examination of the patient. If we should give you any ad-

vice from here it would only be guess work. I hope the bulletin on Prenatal Care will give you some information which will be of use to you, as to the proper care of yourself during pregnancy. I should advise, if possible, your consulting specialists in your own or some large city, as to your own symptoms, and especially as to your boy's eyes. From your description it seems to me that this is a condition which should have expert care, if possible."

Mrs. H.S., Virginia (December 4, 1917)

I am writing this hoping that you will give me some information that will help me with my baby girl. She is eight months old, weighs 25 lbs., seems to be well proportioned for her age, but here's the trouble. Her bowels have been too loose all the time since birth, and most of the time its a greenish looking mucus. Her bowels move from 6 to 12 times a day. I have been to the Dr. time and again. He gives me a pink tablet which I think contains calomel but I can never find out from him what causes this mucus to form. Here, let me say the pink tablets act on the bowels and for a few day's the color of her stools are yellow but *very* thin, then she gets back again as bad as ever with the mucus. I have read every article I could get my hands on, concerning babies, but I can't find any thing about this. I give her lots of attention, bath every day, change from skin out. I nurse her regularly, give her an outing every day. In fact do every thing that I know what to do for health and development, but I am very ignorant concerning babies.

People here in the mountains raise them very rough and call mine a *book* baby, but with doing all I possibly can for her I fear I will not be able to raise her. My *only* other baby born eight years ago started just like this. I was

104   Raising the Baby

advised to wean her at six months, so I took her from the
breast and I never did get a food that agreed with her so at
10 1/2 months she died. The fear that this baby will
continually get worse haunts me day and night. So in
sheer desperation I've written this.

Perhaps its nursing too much causes this mucus. I am a
very hearty eater, have a plentiful milk flow. I milk my
breasts dry before retiring so when she nurses at night she
will not have so much. Then I sometimes wonder if I have
her dressed properly. She wears a flannel shirt. Her outing
pet[t]icoat covers up over her chest, then a gingham dress,
cotton stocking, outing diapers. She is kept very clean.
Please give me some advise concerning this, or if there is
any book on this subject I will gladly send check for same.
Let me add, old folks say my baby has cold on her bowels
that causes this mucus. She has never been down on floor
and I see no way for her to have cold always. Hoping to
get a reply, I am Respt.

She does not have red cheeks, but is rather pale, and
when the mucus is worst, there are circles under her eyes.

*West replies that some of the infant's digestive problems
may be a result of overfeeding.*

Mrs. O.W., Washington (March 17, 1918)
Sirs:—

Would you kindly send me a bulletin on the care of
babies. My baby is breast-fed and now two months old.
[He] is gaining in weight about half a pound a week, but
his bowels are not normal. The movement is greenish
with mucus and cruds; he has as many as six and seven a
day. He is very cross and seems to be in pain especially

before his bowels move. He often screams; he has been
this way from the day I brought him home. He was born
in the hospital. My doctor says there is nothing to do for
it. I have asked him several times and each time he tells
me not to worry as it will affect the quality of the milk.
Still I feel that my baby is not right and want some good
advice. I cannot help but worry and cannot rest, as the
Doctor advises, when baby crys most of the time. He also
sneezes a good deal. I keep the room at a temperature
between 70° and 80° and he is dressed in half wool
flannel.

I give him fresh air by covering up his crib and open the
window. He weighed 6 lb 7 oz at birth and now about 11
lbs.

Thanking you in advance for your advice, I am
sincerely.

Meigs writes that, according to Infant Care, *diarrhea is
often caused by nursing the baby too often or at irregular intervals. She suggests that Mrs. O.W. see a physician.*

Mrs. G.W., Baltimore, Maryland (April 15, 1918)
Dear Sirs.

I have just finished reading an article by Addington
Bruce in the Star Paper of this city about the campaign
that is to be started to save the babies. I am a young
mother and have 3 children aged 4 months, 2 years, and
4 years. Would you please be kind enough to send me two
copies of Mrs. Max West's pamphlets, Prenatal Care and
Infant Care, also any other litera[t]ure that you distribute
among mothers. I should very much like to study up on
the care of babies as I have had trouble with every baby

with malnutrition. I give them the best care I know how
and try to feed them right, but maybe I don't know how to
take care of them properly. I haven't time to run to the
hospitial dispensary every day, as they keep you most all
day, and I would have to neglect the other children while
I took one. The baby 2 years old doesn't walk a step.
What do you think is the cause of this? He is an extremely
heavy child but I think he has the rickets. He doesn't talk
a word either. Could I correspond with some one in your
dept. giving me advise about the Children? Sincerely.
Answer soon.

    *West referred Mrs. G.W.'s case to the Baltimore Babies'
Milk Fund Association. That agency wrote to West after a visiting nurse had talked with Mrs. G.W.: "Mrs. W. does not seem
very eager for the nurse to visit her, she is well informed and is
familiar with all the dispensaries and hospitals of the city, and she
and her family go to them, when it is necessary to have treatment." West replied, "Evidently she is one of those women who
cannot be helped and therefore we may as well dismiss her from
our minds. I assume, however, that you will like to have any
such case referred to you in order that you may sift it."*

Mrs. W.D., Pennsylvania (April 17, 1918)
    Will you please send me these bulletins: Canning
Vegetables in the Home—no 359, Bread and
Breadmaking—no 389, the Home Vegetable Garden—no
225, Dry Fruits and Vegetables—no 481. Inclosed you will
find two three cent stamps for postage.
    P.S. My baby is one year old and is very delicate. She
weighed 9 pounds at birth and weighs only 14 pounds
now. She has only three teeth. I took her to my doctor; he
said she was underfed, so besides giving her the cows milk,

I tried giving her coddled egg every day, but she will not take it. Will you please let me know if egg nog will harm her or tell me of some good food to give her in place of egg? I live in the country and can not see the doctor very often and I fear she will not live. She is so delicate I have been giving her the very best care. She has also had a cough for about five mo[n]th[s] which seems impossiable to cure. She coughs mostly at night. Oblige.

P.S. The baby also has night sweats and some times she sweats for two days at a time no mat[t]er how cool she is dressed. Her urine has the odor of am[m]onia.

West tells Mrs. W.D. that "it is impossible for us to take the responsibility of directing the care of a sick baby" and refers her letter to Dr. H. of the state Division of Child Hygiene. She also asks Mrs. W.D. to send her more information on the child's diet and on bowel and sleeping habits so that she might "suggest some helpful measures to you."

Mrs. W.D. (May 9, 1918)
My Dear Mrs West

Your letter of April the 27th was received and also a letter from Dr. H., May 8th. The baby has four nursings in 24 hours: [at] seven, eleven, three and seven. I give her milk with the addition of mellins food and water, dry toast and strained oatmeal, with a little [w]hole milk, broth and orange juice when I can get it. She eats very little of the toast and broth. Since I have given her the cereal, she has gained a little.

When I weaned her from the breast, I gave her Horlicks Malted milk. I saw baby failing every day. I took her to Dr. K. & he perscribed Mellins food. But still she does not gain as she should.

There is one point which I did not mention in my last letter, but now I am glad to write to you personally and explain to you. My Baby has masturbated since five months old. I had the book of "Infant Care" and tried every possiable way to cure her of this and the cough she has. But I have worked in vain.

I told Dr. K. she masturbated and he could not believe it. So when I positivaly knew she did I could not have the heart to go to another doctor unless it were a specialist that would take interest in her af[f]air. Dr. K. said he never heard of a child under the age of four masturbate. I am certainly very much grieved over her condition as I think this is the reason for her being so delicate.

The baby goes to bed a little after seven and sleeps in her own bed until seven in the morning but coughs frequently. She stays out of doors all day and has every advantage to gain. Now I have taken the opertunity to cor[re]spond with you knowing of your experience. I have given here the whole truth about Baby, hoping you can give me good advice. I would be willing to take her any place, to a specialist or do anything you advise me to do. I will pay any price within my means to have her cured. I will not write to Doctor H. until I hear from you again. Hoping I will hear from you again soon. I am very sincerely yours.

West tells Mrs. W.D. that Dr. H. will visit her.

Mrs. F.D., Quebec (December 18, 1921)
Dear Miss Rude:
Received your welcomed and helpful letter sometime ago. Pardon the awful delay. The reason, was ill with a

severe attack of bronchitis. Am now ever so much better, but still a little weak.

Received bulletins, also dodgers. I surely am very much oblige[d] to you, as it is a great help to me. There is no Infants Clinic in this country, and I surely do miss them. In my home-town, which is Minneapolis, Minnesota, we have several for the rich like the poor. I don't like the doctors out here as they are very old-fashion. They don't believe in [feeding at] any regular intervals, and, believe me, thats what I insist on most firmly. At first I would feed the baby every three hours, but he vomited something awful and the helpful bulletin tells me to lengthen it to every four hrs. Which I have. He vomits less now.

But still one more difficult[y] I have, probably you will help me again. It is about his bowels. I have tried every thing the bulletin says. They will move for two or three days, then stop. First I have given him olive oil (warm), two tablespoon. No results. Orange juice with water. No results, and given before bath. [He] would cry very much too, shortly after [being] given the juice. It is either a Glycerine Suppository or an enema of pure castile soap. I have results. I am afraid for an irritation of the rectum, also inflamation of the bowels. What do you say?

Of course I don't take him out, as I can't afford a sleigh nor carriage, but I sometimes leave him with a kind neighbor near me. And I go for a stroll. Which is not very often as I'm a stranger here in town; my friends are all in M'polis. One true thing I do, I must tell you, is that I think and pine for my hometown. My husband knows it too, but we haven't the necessary funds yet. So I have to brace up and think of something cheerful, which at times seems very hard. Do you suppose that has anything to do?

Baby gains very much; his feeding hours are 10 a.m., 2
p.m., 6 p.m., 6 a.m. [He is] in bed, [a]sleep till 6:30 each
morning. Sometimes he will awake around 2:00 a.m. in
the morning. He is 4 months the 22 of this month.

Speaking of the bowels again, I have also given him
boiled water which is cooled, but I have to slightly sugar it
otherwise he will vomit it or spit it up. Does the sugar do
harm??? He has about 3 to 4 oz every day, and sometimes
after his 6:00 pm feeding he will fall asleep with the
bottle of water. Am I giving him enough water or too
much, as he wets often enough? I make his bowels move
regularly before bath and in the afternoon before his
feeding at 6 at night. If they don't move during the night;
that is, before he awakes for his 6:00 a.m. feeding, he will
cry and double up with pain. I have to give him an enema
for results, and [he] will sleep again till about 8:00 a.m.
[He] stays in his basket till I take him up to bathe. If his
bowels hasn't moved, I have to give him another enema
before bath. Can you help me?

Much I would like to know you, as your just like a
mother to me, as I'm an orphan, only three sisters, two
are married. And they have their own troubles. Ha! Ha!

My husband is a canadien citizen, but I'm going to
make him a good American citizen instead. There's no
country equal to the good old U.S.A. This is my first trip
away from M'polis, and I don't care to travel any more
either. Work is getting so scarce; thats what keeps us from
putting the necessary funds for travel back aside. To tell
the truth, I'm at times to tell the true to the point of
[wondering if we're] ever going back. I can't figure to see
that day. But I still hope, for baby's sake.

Dear Miss Rude pardon me for taking so much of your

time, which no doubt you must be very busy. Words can
not express what I feel for you in my heart. I can only
write that I thank you infinitely for your kindness towards
helping me with my baby. Must close with my best
regards. I am as ever.

*Rude sees no reason to use olive oil for constipation and
suggests that Mrs. F.D. use fruit juice diluted with water instead. She adds that although a glycerine or soap suppository can
be used when necessary, prolonged use causes irritation. Rude
does not recommend enemas except in real emergencies and tells
Mrs. F.D. that it is not necessary that a baby's bowels move
more than once a day. She says Mrs. F.D.'s baby seems to be
gaining well but that if he wakens at night, she could overcome
the problem by nursing him at her own bedtime, nine or ten
o'clock. "This will ensure a long sleep through the rest of the
night and will be best both for you and the baby," she writes. She
adds that it is not good to feed a child sugar, for it establishes a
"habit for sweets."*

Mrs. L.L., Maine (May 23, 1922)
Julia Lathrop:
    Some time ago I recieved one of your publications
entiteled "Child Care: The Preschool Age." I have read
and reread "Child Care" and got so much help from it that
I am asking for your publications "Prenatal Care No. 4"
and also "Infant Care No. 8." I should be very grateful if
you have anything else that you think would help me. We
live on a farm and I do *all* my own work. My husband
works hard all the time and we are very happy. We have
six children, the oldest nine years and the youngest one
year. We are expecting another baby in November and I

would like to care for baby so as to give him good teeth. The two oldest haven't any enamel on their teeth at all and one of the girls teeth look kind of yellow and I am afraid they will be like the two oldest boys. The other boy age six and a half and the oldest girl age five and baby age one all got beautiful teeth. But the other three have teeth like mine were. They all have brushes and begin taking care of their teeth when two years old. This is not very concise for a business letter but hope you will forgive me.

P.S. For conveniences we have a separator and water pumped to the sink and a sewing machine. The two oldest boys were operated on last summer for tonsils and adenoids and they are gaining and look and feel *so* much better. The next two a boy and a girl, *must* be operated on for the same this summer. D.'s are affecting his hearing and the girl's throat is nearly full. So if you can give me any suggestions about their care I would be very thankful. Of course we must economize just all we can but I consider it poor economy at the expense of the little ones' health.

Mrs. W.F., Kansas City, Missouri (received August 1, 1925)

More than a yr. ago, I wrote for information on raising my boy, who is now 3 yr. 8 mo. old. For more than a yr. he has been troubled with Colds. First in his ears, now I believe he has catarrah of the nose. And next, I expect, is suggestions to have the tonsils removed. Most of this is caused by improper housing at times & food. I had no work part [of] the time and coulden't hire the right place for him. . . . Altho the parties [who ran the child

care] might have had the right food, they catered to his
whims or his first demand, & would even hand him
weinies just before breakfast, toasties & lots of sugar in
winter, maybe 3 or 4 sausages, sauerkraut, or pork &
beans for supper [with] syrup on top of it.

He then developed a terrible cold all thru his system.
Even his eyes begin to look bad & I treated them with
Argarol. Now I want to know if you will suggest some diet
to build him up, as I can count his ribs, and at times he
looks blue about his eyes & nose, and pale faced. For a yr.
his teeth have been decaying. [He] has several to fill.

We live near the city hospital and the court lady who
visits us suggests I get the children in [foster] homes or
institutions. [She] says she could arrange to have our teeth
fil[l]ed at the hospital, and I took the boy over and find
out they do not do work of that kind there. If I try at
other public places they could gather up a few diseases
waiting in the crowds [for] our turn. [We waited] 3 hrs.
the other day.

I had the baby looked at by a common physician. We
were advised to move out of [our] place on the childrens
behalf. Well, we moved into a room heated by a leaking
gas heater. [We had to go] outside into a cold rooming
house for eats a few awful blustery cold days before we
could arrange to find any other place, & then we didn't
get where the gas was piped correctly. It was hard on my
eyes. My baby of 2 months had red streaks . . . in the
White [of her eyes] for several days, then began holding
her head to one side, and [was] troubled with flem in
throat & gag[g]ed. . . . [Her] right ear had a bad odor. At
[the] Hospital they advised 1/8 tablet aspirin 3 times a
day, swab[b]ed the ears with a tooth pick wrapped in

cotton & put in ear medicine containing alcahol. I had
been putting warm boric acid water in [them]. . . . She
coughs now. We pay $25.00 month for our 2 rooms. I
don't believe children should be raised in rooms heated by
gas. *And* I believe there should be laws against heating
rooms with gas not correctly piped for the general health
of the people. It might lessen the no. of tonsil removals in
school children. . . .

Will you send me some advise on the subjects of raising
my children? The boy was born July 18, 1921. The girl
Nov. 12th, 1924. Would you advise us to go to a dental
college, where they fill teeth by students cheap? I hear
that at the City hospital every thing is run by politicians,
and we do more waiting than anything else.

Will cod liver oil tablets be good for the children? And
tomato juice for 4 months old baby? I have been trying to
learn what different foods do for the body. . . . We live
near a library. Can you suggest a certain book that would
be somewhat complete on that subject?

I have a father at the State Hospital who has been
helping for years to provide food stuffs & helping 6 hrs. [a]
day for himself & inmates. We have payed also a few yrs
$20 month. They wanted us to pay for every article of
clothing, even to the shoe leather he trod out working. If
we were well enough to do, [we] could furnish him with
things to work with [that] he likes, a radio too, a Victrola,
a car to take him in rides etc. We would gladly care for
him in my home and I believe he would be all right and
happy.

They Brought Him
to the Door in His
Little Casket

Even though death rates were substantially higher for poor
families, women from all class and ethnic backgrounds suffered the loss of their children. These letters show that, like
the "experts" in the Children's Bureau, many of the mothers who lost children attributed their deaths to ignorance
and inadequate health care. Although the letters reflect
women's anger at incompetent physicians, they also document their remarkable trust in the Children's Bureau. Even
women who criticized sections of *Infant Care* expressed
their appreciation for the bulletin, frequently recommend-
ing changes in the pamphlet so that others might be spared
similar pain.

Mrs. L.W., Iowa (January 17, 1916)
Dear Sir:
    Will you please send me "Infant Care" by Mrs. Max
West. Also the book on "Prenatal Care." I would like to
ask your opinion on my case. I gave birth to a 11 lb baby
three weeks ago; the baby was dead when it was borned. It
was borned double. Do you think it could of been turned
and saved, or what is your opinion? Maybe you don't ans
such questions but I thot it would n't do any harm to ask
you. Your's Rept.

Meigs answers, "I should be very glad indeed to answer your question if I could, but I am afraid I do not quite understand it. You say that the baby was born double. I do not understand exactly what you mean by that, and therefore I can not tell you whether anything could have been done to prevent it. If you care to give me any more details perhaps I would be able to tell you more." There is no record of Mrs. L. W.'s response.

Mrs. W.D., Brooklyn, New York (September 10, 1917)
My Dear Mrs. M. West.

I have read about you and your wonderful pamphlets "Prenatal Care" and "Infant Care" in the Farm Journal and I am asking you to please send me both books and I hope you will read my letter. I am a lover of babies and yet I can't seems to have them. I am married 11 yrs last July and would have six children and am about to become a mother again which I almost fear. I have now but 2 out of six, one boy 9 yrs and one 6 yrs.

A year ago last Mar. I gave birth to a beautiful fat boy and it lived but 3 days. The Drs. claimed the baby had a leaking heart; he died in convulsions. I would like to know if the injection the *woman* gave him of soap & water threw him in these convulsions as he just moaned like a pigeon & his whole body shook after that & at night he was dead. This was the first time I became pregnant in 4 yrs and you can imagine how glad & happy I was, only instead of having him at my breast, the third day they brought him to the door in his little casket. My heart was broke. I wish that I too was taken, as I suffer terrible with my head during the 9 mths and then I am always in labor from 10 to 12 hrs at a stretch before I can

bear my babies. It was only 3 mts again until I was to
become a mother again, so I had another babe the next
Feb., this making 2 in 1 yrs. I raised him until he was 1 yr
and 11 days. He was an angel, never cried, to[o] good I
guess to be left on earth. I washed and put his night
drawers on and put him to bed well & healthy. He played
about the floor that night, laughing and as happy as could
be. I nursed him at 3 o'clock in the morning and I awoke
at 7 am and found him dead along side of me. You can
think how I feel. I cry night and day for my big fat baby,
[taken] from me like that.

I try and live a good honest life and my home is my
heaven and babies are my idols. I love them but I am
afraid something will happen to this one again. I am stout
and as a rule healthy. I can't understand why my babies
should have weak hearts; that is why I am asking for your
books. Maybe I can be spared that terrible long labor and
my babies will be spared. I pray God to [help] me, as the
home seems so cold & dreary without a babys voice.
Good-by, with Love & wishes of Good luck to you, I
remain.

West writes, "I am very sorry to hear that you have had
such an unfortunate time with your babies. Have you been
under the care of a competent physician yourself and have you
had your babies under such care? The questions you raise are so
entirely medical ones, that it would be impossible for me to give
any opinion upon them and I can only urge that you go to the
best doctor you can find immediately and give him an opportunity to study your case and to try to help you.

"I notice in your letter that you speak of nursing a baby over a
year old at 3 : 00 o'clock in the morning and also that he was in
bed with you. A child of that age should not be nursed or fed at

night, but should sleep straight through and also should sleep in a crib by himself, never with his mother or an older person.

"Do you know about the Infant Welfare Stations of New York City? There are such stations in Brooklyn where you can take your baby for free examination by excellent doctors and after your baby is born it would be a great help to you I am sure, if you would take him regularly to the station nearest you. With best wishes, believe me, very sincerely yours."

Mrs. W.D., Boston area, Massachusetts (June 22, 1918)
My Dear Miss Lathrop:

I have just finished attending the lectures given in Boston during a baby welfare week. . . . You are no doubt a busy department but I would like to tell you how interested I am in baby and child welfare and why. Just two years ago, after five years of married life, we became the proud parents of our first baby, a boy. Four months later we buried our baby and it was then that I knew how helpless I was when it came to knowing what a mother should know. My baby was sacrificed thru mere ignorance. This happened in the capitol of Illinois and money or efforts were not spared to save him. I soon found that not only mothers of large families knew nothing about the scientific care of babies, but the best Doctors in the city knew less. I could not nurse my baby, and he just faded away, never gaining, or rather losing weight all the time on the many foods which the different Doctors tried.

Before my baby came I read and studied every thing I could on baby care and I knew about regular feeding. And of course being people of clean living, I felt our baby had every chance. Our home was clean and sanitary and far more luxurious than lots of children. But when I had to stand by and see my baby slowly starve I made up my mind I'd fight the world but what I'd find out some way to teach people more about babies. Since that time I've read and studied every thing I could get. I've visited public clinics and hospitals, I've attended baby welfare lectures. But I find so few people who are ready to believe in better baby care, and most of all the mothers with families. They are ready as a rule to laugh in your face.

I realize that a wonderful work is being done. And I know that in the future more wonderful things will be done. I know that it can't be done in a day but oh! lets make them understand as soon as we can. I want every thing I can get to read, all the help I can get from you or anyone else. And I only wish I could take up the work of promoting baby welfare. At present my husband is an officier in the Navy doing his bit and I consider this no time for us to risk what we have suffered in the past. But when this war is over and I am sure of the proper help to start my baby in life I mean to have babies, not a baby, and I mean to raise them to be good healthy Americans and I hope they will never know what an experience it has been to live in this time of suffering babies.

Any advice I could get in regard to expectant mothers would be gladly received. I was ill during all my pregnancy and in the hospital for a long while and at the time of confinement I was unusually ill and I have always felt that it was lack of proper care. I know our doctors are good but when abnormal things come up they do not always give them enough attention. If we could all be in the big hospitals in the big cities we would have a better chance. But so few can do that.

I hope I have not told my story out of place. I am so anxious to learn and to help others to learn more of this much needed work. Very respectfully.

Mrs. F.W., Michigan (June 25, 1918)
Dear Madam:
     May I make a suggestion concerning the bulletin "Infant Care"? If it be of help in preparing future editions, my babies death will not have been altogether in vain.
     He was our first baby so I referred to my bulletin a great deal in taking care of him. The biggest mistake was probably made by our doctor, who advised against weaning, altho my milk was poor in both quantity and quality. But the use of soap stick and of lime water after weaning (at nine mo.), as "Infant Care" advises, made him more constipated than he would otherwise have been.
     We took him, last August, to a baby specialist of Detroit, Dr. B., who said he was normal in every way except for chronic inflamation of the bowels, and attendant ills due to previous attacks of indigestion and the following reduced feeding. He advised against the use of lime water for normal children.
     Our baby had not had an unaided movement of the bowels for more than a year when he died this June, at the age of two and a half years, [too] worn out to cut his last two baby teeth.
     I'm sorry to have intruded my troubles upon you, but for the sake of other babies all over the land, wouldn't it be better to warn against the indiscriminate use of the soap stick (it is so easy to see its advantages without thinking of the dangers), and to recommend the use of lime water only upon a doctor's advice?

"The Care and Feeding of Children" by Dr. Holt does
not agree with the bulletin on those two points.

The bulletin was a big help to me in other ways and I
should have followed it more closely than I did. We now
have a happy fat baby boy who is profiting by what his
mother has learned. Very respectfully yours.

Mrs. C.A., Missouri (November 11, 1924)
Dear Mrs West:—

I have just returned from the hospital, after having
given birth to a beautiful baby boy weighing seven pounds
and eleven ounces—but we lost him—and the purpose of
this letter is to ascertain why this happened. I will give
you complete details regarding my own health etc., &
perhaps you can give out additional information in your
very helpful publication that will eliminate much sorrow
. . . .

I was under the care of a very competent physician &
surgeon during the entire period before baby came & was
in perfect health at the time of birth. The cause of the
baby's death was due to the location of the umbilical cord
which was under the little left arm, and as the child was
born, the breath of course was cut off, permitting the
child to breathe through its lungs. The lungs, naturally,
filled up with the surrounding fluid, and altho the baby's
little heart beat for twenty minutes, the combined efforts
of the attending physicians assisted by three nurses in one
of the best equipped hospitals in this section of the
country failed to induce the baby to breathe. Every means
known to science was used for a period of 2 hours in an
effort to bring back the little life, but to no avail.

Now the cord was unusually long, approximately 2 yards

in length, and what I am anxious to know is what
probably caused the unusual length in the cord & if
science has discovered anything that will eliminate the
dangers this cord has relative to the birth of the child.
Also if it is possible to ascertain the position of the cord
before birth through the aid of an xray or some other
means known to science. I drove my car from the very
first & within possibly a month before baby was born with
the consent of my physician. Could this have had any
effect, in your opinion?

I read & re-read your publication #4 and followed
instructions religiously. In fact, I took such splendid care
of myself, that I had not even the slightest doubt as to the
outcome, regarding either the baby or myself and of course
the shock was almost more than we could stand. Instead
of the darling baby boy we have only a beautiful memory.

In closing, I want to say that the only consolation we
can find is in the expectancy of another little life, and any
information you can give regardless of cost will be greatly
appreciated. Perhaps in your next publication it might be
possible to devote a section to the "Umbilical Cord,"
thereby eliminating not only the dangers attendant to
childbirth, but a great deal of sorrow and misery in the
world.

I shall wait anxiously for a letter from you which will
enlighten me on this mysterious & fascinating subject of
obstetrics. I am just twenty-eight years of age & having
once passed through this beautiful but sad experience, I
hope to devote my entire life to the rearing & care of a
healthy family. Please do not hesitate to give me full
information regarding the Prenatal Care—if you desire
any cooperation, I will be more than glad to assist you,
through detailed information regarding my own personal
experience. Sincerely yours.

Hull replies that Bureau publications can cover only hygiene, not accidents of pregnancy and labor. She tells Mrs. C.A. that her doctor is the guide and that she can be sure there was nothing she could have done. Later, she sends her a reading list on obstetrics.

Mrs. S.L., Louisiana (August 12, 1926)

Am writing to you to see if it is not possible to put out another Bulletin of information (or have added to your book on "Prenatal Care" more information for ignorant & expected mothers) that is [on] the danger of an instrument birth to a child—what to do with a child when seriously injured by instruments—that is, to take it to a hospital & have it's little head operated on at once, while its little head is just cartilage, & its little brain not yet commencing to develope. Also explain the new method of operating on the mother & taking the child, thus avoiding such injuries & placing if possible these bulletins in [the] hands of nurses & Drs. to be given to their maternity patients.

I am begging the Department of Labor to try & get Drs. & nurses to take more interest in maternity work, as the life of one neglected child is such a costly experience for a ignorant mother & father. I do not want any father & mother to suffer what we have thro ignorance. [That] is why am writing you. We never knew of the danger of an instrument birth. We never knew the child could be taken by an operation. We never knew what to do with our child after it was hurt, until too late & the Drs. [we] had did not seem to know either. Until it was too late.

Our Darling suffered 20 whole long months, to be operated on too late, & it cost her her life. Our only child leaving us, [our] hearts breaking from the suffering only a

mother & father who worship[p]ed their child can know.
So please try & help others through your department all
you can & keep them from making the horrible mistake
we made, & [from] the loss of the one whose place can
never be filled. & what makes it so much worse is the fact
it was so unnecessary, the seeming murder from pure
ignorance. So please try & add this most necessary
information for the ignorant to your helpful Bulletins.
Cant you possibly do this? Am so anxious to know! & it is
so badly needed. I speak from a heart full of aching
practical experience, a loved one lost through ignorance.
"The *one*" whose place *can never be filled.*

Do please try to help others? Surely such Bulletins
should be in the homes of every married family, especially
the young married couples who must get so much from
experience. We never knew until too late & the
experience is entirely too costly. Is all. Sincerely.

P.S. Please send me a copy of these or this bulletin soon
as you put it out for public service & benefit, *wont you
please?* Our babys head was badly hurt, the instruments
crushed its little head in front—the forehead above the
eyes—& it left pressure causing 20 months of suffering to
be operated on too late. Please furnish the necessary
information for such ignorance to expectant mothers you
can reach thro your Bulletins.

*Alice Flood writes, "We are indeed sorry to hear of your
great grief and sympathize with you most deeply. No matter
what is done, whether a Caesarean section or an instrumental
labor, there are always a certain number of babies who die from
birth injuries. This state of affairs is being constantly worked
upon and studied by the medical profession. There are numerous
articles on birth injuries but these are all in medical libraries and
are entirely for the use of the doctors. They could not be put into*

books which would be intelligible to the general public. Your doctor without doubt did the very best possible for you under the
conditions existing at the time of your labor."

Mrs. G.B., Missouri (February 11, 1932)
    Some months back I recieved a parental book and
Some baby patterns from U.S. Department of Labor
Childrens Bureau, Washing[ton] D.C. I recieved them
about a month before my baby was born. It was born the
16th of oct. and died the 24 of october. [It] was marked by
Something. An open cavity in back of the head had
Something Stuck up away into the bone; the place looked
like the intestines of a chicken or something similar to it.
I don't [k]no[w] how I happen to mark it, only one thing I
remembered seeing. I had to go thru a pasture at my work
and accidently Saw a cow giving birth to a calf when I was
allmost 3 months a long, and I'm wondering if it was
marked by that. [The baby's head] had [two] little skins
hanging that I thought resembled the calf's [two] front
feet the way they hung, and a bulge that resembled its
nose. Tell me where it is possible that one can be marked
this way or not? Some of the papers say they cant be
marked. My baby was the Stoutest baby I ever had except
that when the blood and water seeped out it was down
smooth with the head and it died soon after.
    I thank you for the patterns and letters I received, as a
mother can't have too much advice. And I have a niece I
wish you would Send the baby patterns and parental book
to right away. I think She is a bout 6 months along. So
pl[e]ase here is her address. She is only 16 yrs old. I will
appreciate any good advice. Yours truly. My baby only
lived 8 days.

Blanche Haines writes, "I am sorry to hear that you lost your baby, and I assure you that the sights you saw had nothing to do with the fact that the baby was born with defective bone development. You did not mark your baby; that would not be possible."

Chapter Three

Motherhood: All Work and No Money

*I Am Busy All Day
But My Work
Is Never Done*

Most childrearing advice in the 1910s and 1920s assumed that mothers had household help and the leisure time to devote to childrearing, but few of the women who wrote to the Children's Bureau had much time for child training. Housework and farm chores were full-time jobs that depleted their time and energy. Women's letters to the Children's Bureau reflect their concern with time; several of the correspondents apologize for taking too much of the Bureau's "valuable" time. In *Infant Care* and in her answers to letters from her readers, Mary West demonstrated her understanding of women's lack of time. Her response to Mrs. N.W. shows how well she knew the difficulty of arranging a daily schedule that allowed time to enjoy the children as well as to complete the household chores.

Mrs. M.T., Texas (June 23, 1916):

I wish to thank you for the two booklets you sent to my son's wife & I last year, the second monograph you call it. Would you be kind enough to send one of the first number of this series entitled "Prenatal Care" to both my daughter-in-law and I? I would also like the next booklet about training, etc. from the second year on. If you have such please send it to me as well as the 1st book. Is there no charge for these books? If any, how much is it?

They are very helpful and I should like to have the whole series if I could get them. I have had nine children, but there is much in these booklets I never heard, no, nor even thought of. I have one little girl nearly 10, but I do not know how or what to teach her hardly: in fact, I have so much to do, I have no time to teach, only to scramble through some way. If you have booklets which will be helpful to me, I would thank you to tell me of them or just send them. My mother taught *me nothing*. I am *still* paying the penalty of ignorance. Thanking you again, I am yours sincerely.

Julia Lathrop responds that the government appropriated funds to send the books free of charge to people "who can make use of them. I need not say that we are very much pleased by the testimony to their usefulness which your letter contains." She asks Mrs. M.T. whether the Bureau can publish her letter if it conceals her name and address. "Of course, the Bureau can only know at first hand how people feel about its publications through its correspondence. Your wise and generous letter is one that would help many people."

Mrs. M.T. (July 18, 1916)

Your letter of July 8 came to me as a delightful surprise. I do not see *what* I could have said in my letter that could be of benefit to any one else, but "Uncle Sam" is welcome to *any & all service I can ever give*; and you can most certainly publish my letter. I came to Texas when only six years old from London, England, and I am proud to be one of the Old Timers of 1883. Yours sincerely.

Mrs. N.W., Seattle, Washington (March 4, 1920)

Dear Mrs. Lathrop,

Would I be intruding too much upon your valuable time if I bring you my personal problems and ask your assistance? I would be greatly indebted to you if you would advise me or send me helpful literature.

I am a *busy* mother of three dear babies—aged 3 years, 20 months and 3 months. I am obliged to do all my work and we have not the conveniences and modern utilities that I wish we could afford. I am up-to-date in the care of my babies, reading and following the best literature on the care of babies. The help I need is in planning my work—a work schedule or something to aid me in the daily routine. I do the very best I can. I am busy all day and all evening but my work is never done—I am tired enough to drop when night comes and in the morning look with dread upon the day ahead of me. I want to play with my babies, I want to have time to love them and laugh with them. I have wanted babies for years and now, when Im so tired and with unfinished work every where I turn, I could scream at their constant prattle. I love them until it hurts and know that, when they are out of their babyhood, I can never forgive myself for not making more of these precious years.

Is there not some way that I can do all these scientific and hygienic duties for babies, keep our house up in proper fashion and still have time to rock and play with my babies? What of all my housework and baby-care could best be left undone? I do not ask time for myself but it would be nice to have a short period during the evening in which to read as I feel that I am growing narrow with no thoughts other than my household.

Thanking you for all the past helps your department has rendered me. Sincerely.

In a two-page letter, West tells Mrs. N.W. that Julia Lathrop asked her to respond to the letter because she had several children. "It is most difficult to arrange any one else's life, or even to make suggestions that would be helpful," she writes apologetically. "If we could talk the matter over, and I could learn from you your usual routine, I am sure I could point out to you several places where you could save your strength.

"In regard to your household, I should suggest what you have probably already accomplished, namely, cutting down to the mere essentials in your cooking and cleaning; also in putting off on any one else available some of the hard work, especially any very heavy work that you feel takes a great deal out of you.

"In regard to the care of three little children under three years of age: this alone is a full day's job for any one woman, and the only way that you can accomplish it and do the essential things for your household, is to systematize their hours and run their meals, naps, hours of play, and night sleep on a regular schedule." West further advises Mrs. N.W. that she put her children on the same nap schedule, try to avoid washing dishes more than once or twice a day, and arrange nap and feeding times so that she can lie down. Finally, she advises having all three children in

bed before her own supper. "*If you have not tried putting away your children at six o'clock, you have no idea what a relief it will be to you. It can be done; I have done it myself with three boys, and no mother who knows the satisfaction of having the care of her children cease before her own evening meal, and the quiet comfort of a still household in the evening, would fail to immediately begin the training necessary to make it possible.*

"*If you can have your time after supper to yourself, and your one hour of rest in the early afternoon, I believe you will find your energy for the day's work considerably greater and your enjoyment of your children very much heightened.*

"*I hesitated to offer these suggestions, because I know how impossible they might seem to you and to me if I understood your situation more clearly. I hope you will write me more details of your problem, and let me be of any service in my power.*"

Mrs. H.P., Kansas (July 28, 1921). Copy enclosed in correspondence from Florence Sherbon, Kansas Department of Health, to Julia Lathrop (August 24, 1921) "for public use in the Sheppard-Towner Campaign."[1]
Dear Doctor Sherbon:—

You can not imagine how much I have enjoyed the Course.[2] As soon as I received it I lay down and never stopped until I read it through. It is splendid, and if every woman could follow each lesson to the letter there would be less suffering. But how are we going to convince our

1. Sherbon also enclosed a letter from Mrs. A.G. of Kansas, which is reproduced later in this chapter.
2. The correspondence course consisted of nine monthly letters sent to women during their pregnancies. Distributed by the state departments of health, these courses were among the most popular means of providing information on prenatal care.

families that such care is necessary? Of course the children can be taught these things, but the husbands and our mothers think it is foolishness to take such care of ourselves.

Oh! if I could only follow your advice, but it seems that my work gets harder instead of easier. Just now I am expecting threshers—about 30 men for two days, and, while I will have help, I have to go ahead and get things ready for others. And I do not know just when my time is up, as I have never menstruated since my last baby was born two years ago. I am so tired! If I could only rest a while, but I don't see any chance. I have had my children so fast and have had so much to do I am worn out. There are seven in the family now and I am only 26. What will I be like in ten years more, if I live?

Do you think it proper to explain to children where they come from and the science of life? I have told my stepson, age 18, all of these things and how he should take care of himself, and also how he should treat girls and how much suffering there was to childbirth, and I was very much criticized by some of the family.

I must close. I am taking up your valuable time and am losing much time of my own. Thank you for all the help and the good you are doing, not only for myself but others.

There Is No Way of Buying the Most Needy Things

Although women both on farms and in cities faced grueling work that weakened their health, families often felt that medical and prenatal care was a luxury. Even women who had convinced their families of the importance of such care found that it was difficult to obtain because of distance, poverty, or lack of household help. These letters document poor women's resourcefulness, perseverance, hope, and despair. Hearsay about the Children's Bureau baby-saving campaign and rumors of legislation that would limit medical bills led some women to ask the government for help. Although the Children's Bureau was powerless to offer any material assistance, its staff referred many of the correspondents to local charities or state departments of health. These referrals sometimes resulted in a call from a visiting nurse. Unfortunately, the Children's Bureau files contain no record of these visits.

Mrs. M.R., Idaho (January 4, 1916)
Dear Madame.
    I would like to know if your people can give me a answer on this. What I am to do I dont know. I am living 25 miles away from any Doctor. We have 4 small children, my Husband is only making 1.35 a day, and every thing is

so high it takes all he makes to keep our babys in cloth[e]s
and food, as we have ev[e]ry thing we put in our mouths
to buy. I am looking for the stork about the 19 of aprial,
and all I can do is to get a few outing [flannel] slips and a
few Di[a]pers. So hear is what I would like for yous to
answer if you can: how am I going to get 35 dollar to have
a doctor, for he will not come for less and not unless we
have the cash. Talk about better babys, when a mother
must be like some cow or mare when a babys come. If she
lives, all wright, and if not, Just the same. The nearest
one that lives is 1 mile and a 1/2 and my oldest child is
9 years old. My husband only comes home onest a week,
that is on saterday. I have my own wood to cut by my self
so how can there be better babys when they must come in
to this world like a calf or colt I would like to know.

So please answer me if you can. You may send me a
copie of Bulletin and if I live [through] it, then I will try
to [follow] it as close as I can. Yours truly, answe[r] at
[once].

Lathrop responds, "I have read your letter with a great deal
of sympathy and earnestly wish that I knew how to be of service
to you. Sometime I hope that our country will be so organized
that there will be a doctor and nurse stationed at various points,
so that no one can be twenty-five miles from a physician.

"I am sending you . . . bulletins which were written by Mrs.
Max West of this Bureau, who is herself the mother of five children. They were all very young when she was left a widow and
had to begin to earn a living for them and for herself. That took
courage, and I can see plainly that your life requires great courage too."

Mrs. W.S., Brooklyn, New York (January 30, 1918)
Dear Madam,
    I read this mornings article in the New York
American about the campaign to save babies. I fear my
baby will be born too soon to have such wonderful help as
you propose. My babies come fast and where I am going to
meet the Doctors bills I cannot see. I have a daughter one
year old this Jan. and we have had little else but Doctors
bill[s] in the past 3 years. i cannot get enough bed
clothing for that time without going in debt. I have a very
good husband but he has such poor health. He makes
20.70 a week, but to buy coal at 30c a small bag and oil at
14c a gallon, and other things so high we can not save a
penny. I dont like to tell my husband all I fear as he has
enough to bear. My husband felt it is his duty to take out a
Liberty Bond and we are paying for it 1.00 a week. I
would like to ask him to give it up, but dont seem to be
able to do so. I can and would gladly do sewing to earn
some money but can find no work like that in these times.
Can you show me a way out or a way I can help my self? I
expect my baby the first of March. I hope I have not done
anything wrong in writing to you like this. I am very
respectfully.

Mrs. W.S. (February 4, 1918)
Dear Miss Lathrop,
    Your letter of the first just received and I thank you
very much for your kind attention in the matter. I would
be very thankful for any help you would suggest. The
doctor I have been treated by up to date intends to charge
me $15.00 which I will find it quite hard to meet. I could

not go to a hospital very well as I would not know what to do with my year old baby. So if you can help me to get treatment for a less amount I would be very grateful to you. Thanking you again, I am very respectful[l]y. Would you kindly send me the books you send out on the care of children?

With "very great sympathy and respect," Lathrop responds to the first letter by referring Mrs. W.S. to the Babies Welfare Association. Correspondence with that organization reveals that an agent talked with her about how she could secure a nurse and provide temporary care for her one-year-old, and a wealthy woman agreed to donate bedding and baby clothing.

Mrs. A.G., Kansas (August 10, 1921). Copy enclosed in correspondence from Florence Sherbon, Kansas Department of Health, to Julia Lathrop (August 29, 1921)[3]

Dear Madam:

I took your correspondence course last winter and enjoyed it very much although I have been a mother three times and expect to be again as am pregnant three months now. Maybe you have something for me or that might help me in some way, so [I] thot that I would drop you a line.

We are a poor family and live in western Kansas and [are] heavily in debt, so this ordeal is hard for me at present. But what I would like to ask you is if a poor mother can get any county or state aid. My teeth are badly

3. See also the letter from Mrs. H.P., Kansas, which appears earlier in this chapter.

in need of dental work, and [I have] no money to pay the
bill and the doctor bill worries me too. The doctor we
have gone to is so high I don't see how we can afford it.
We owe $125 in doctor bills in another county that have
been running for some time, and I dread any more until
back ones are paid.

Isn't there a law in Kansas that unless a confinement
case is obstetrical the limit charge is $15 and if obstetrical
the limit is $25? He says he charges $25 for a confinement
case and $1.00 mileage which would make a total of $37
for us for doctor bill, besides a nurse or lady to nurse and
do the work too. But if you know anything about such
things you know the mother and babe are sadly neglected
if the nurse has all the house work to do too.

We are very much disappointed to go through this so
soon again because I have been in such poor health after
the other two last ones came, and my heart and lungs are
bad anyway. I had scarlet fever and flu a year ago in
January and February which left those organs much weaker
but after coming out here I gained and felt almost O.K.
again, until I became pregnant and it seems all that I had
built up in the last year is sliding back again.

Does the county doctor tend to such cases and look to
the community for his money? It looks like we ought to
be able to do and care for such things without asking for
help, but you know there are just lots and lots of mothers
in my fix that just drag along and worry because they have
no way of buying the most needy things at such a time and
are too proud to find out if there is any way to get help.
My husband thinks it's awful to get help in any way
besides paying for it, but when I know he is not financially
able to help, I don't see why I should suffer if there is any

way to help me, as any mother or doctor knows at that time a mother needs the best of care in every way. And it's because I have always had to work too soon after childbirth that I am broken down now.

I will see what I hear from you before going into details any more. Hoping you will not think it too trifling a matter to interest you and will answer me as soon as possible. Yours truly.

Mrs. S.D., California (September 7, 1921). Letter written to the *Ladies' Home Journal*; copy sent to the Children's Bureau (September 19, 1921).
Re: D.D., formerly of ———;
Age: 21 months of age on August 20, 1921;
Weight: 24 1/2 lbs.

As we have moved and do not know yet when we will get our freight, I thot I had better make out a report to you as best I can without your blank.[4] We have been moving around and camping for two months, but D has only had one sick spell and that lasted a couple of hours on the train, and I believe was caused by drinking the ice water, which was all the water we could get on the train or even at the stations. The last night on the train we had to put him to bed crying for water.

At present, I am feeding him baker's bread, canned milk and peanut butter. I give him a little meat and soup and stew, puddings and all the fruit I can get. He wont eat

4. Women's magazines, like the Children's Bureau and state health departments, distributed a variety of forms on which women could record their infants' height, weight, diet, and other related information.

green vegetables but likes potatoes and onions. Sometimes I have nothing to feed him but macaroni and tomatoes. We cannot get much fresh fruit and vegetables. When I can get them, I give him an orange a day. I can't get good butter and have no way to keep it, if I could. I have had to throw two half pounds away already in an attempt to keep it. When we first came to California, he had rather loose bowels but his bowels seem to be all right now and, in fact, I have to give him prunes. As far as I can remember, he has gained in weight and his face and limbs seem to be filling out. He has sixteen teeth.

I expect the new baby the first of next month, and as you told me I could ask you any questions about it, I will take that liberty. Can you give me any information on how to deliver the baby myself? My husband lost his job, with about a thousand other men in the Navy Yard due to the decrease of the Navy appropriations, and as we could not make our payments, we lost our home and furniture and everything we had. My husband got work down here but only worked five days when he fractured his spine and was laid up for some time. He had no insurance to cover the hospital at charges [of] six dollars a day, and as my husband is only making $3.50 per day, part of which we must send for the support of my mother-in-law, it will be impossible to go to the hospital or have a nurse or midwife here as we are only camping and living in a shack and tent. Nor can I find anyone to take care of my boy. I am five miles from [a town] and over a mile from any neighbor and have no means of communicating with either a doctor or neighbor when I get sick, unless it should happen in the night when my husband was home and then, I suppose, I would have the baby before he could get to the nearest neighbor.

My only neighbors are the snakes, lizzards, squirrels, and rats whose very presence has only made me so nervous that I jump a foot if I hear a leaf rustle in the wind. We carry all the drinking water for three blocks and I take all my washing two blocks down to the creek and then have to carry the wet wash home. I am a stranger in a strange land here so have no one to call on for help. I wrote Miss Lathrop of Washington, D.C. in reference to the Sheppard-Towner Maternity Bill but she informs me that the bill has not gone thru yet. She advised me to write the Child Health Dept. of California but Dr. W. hasn't even answered my letter. I thank you so much for your kindness and helpful information you have given me. If you can give me any information as to self-delivery, I shall certainly appreciate it. Sincerely.

Grace Abbott writes Mrs S.D. and the Ladies' Home Journal *that the Child Health Department of California has arranged for the local women's club to handle Mrs. S.D.'s case.*

Mrs. A.F., Arkansas (July 15, 1927)
Dear Doctors
After reading an article in the Southern Ruralist advising every Prospective Mother to write to you I thought I would write. I am expecting a new baby about Oct 24th. Am 35 year old. Have had four children. The youngest is 9 years old. I was operated on last November a year ago [and] had the right Ovrie taken out. The Dr said it was very bad. Two months previous to that time I had been treated 2 and 3 times a week for an ulcerated condition, so all in all I am not very strong at best. We live on a farm so of course I have lots of work to do. I

would like to go to the Hospital for Confinement but Circumstances will not allow that, as we, like lots of others, have had more than one crop failure, so money is too scarce. So any advise you can give me will be greatly appreciated by both my self and my Husband. He is a great deal older than myself, being 61. So we are looking forward to great things for our Baby. So thanking you for your letter of advice, I am yours very truly.

Viola Russell Anderson sends Mrs. A.F. copies of the bulletins and urges her to see a physician.

Mrs. D.B., Pennsylvania (May 19, 1932)
Dear Childrens Bureau

I am an expectant mother and am interested in the information you can give me for the expectant mother. I have one child 22 months old but I was then financially able to go to the hospital. We now can not afford much medical aid But dread to go under with only unskilled nurse. Respectfully.

Frances Rothert replies that she is sending a public health nurse to visit Mrs. D.B. The nurse will help plan care during confinement that is within her budget.

My Heart Aches
for the Poor Children

Although most of the letters to the Children's Bureau were written by mothers seeking help for themselves, a few were from middle-class women who sought to aid those less fortunate than themselves. The child-welfare work of the Bureau depended on the support of mothers' clubs and parent/teacher associations. Middle-class mothers distributed literature, established well-baby clinics, and brought visiting nurses to poor areas; single women like Miss A.R. became nurses or social workers themselves. In contrast to poor women, who claimed that they needed more money to raise healthy children, most of these middle-class women considered education the more pressing need.

Miss A.R., New Jersey (March 7, 1915)
My dear Miss Lathrop:—
    Your book on infant care has just come to me through one of our W.C.T.U. woman of our village. In the "Transmittle Letter" mention is made of another book "Prenatal Care." I would like very much to see it. It sounds like something I have felt the need of for my prospective mothers. At that time they would be more interested and more apt to read and study understandingly and ask intelligent questions of things they did not know that could be explained to them.
    We need something in these rural communities to help the people that do not have the opportunities of those in the cities to help them to better ideals, they are sadly in need of education, some of them in many lines. They never get away from home, know little or nothing of the world outside of their own, and it is by accident that they come in touch with any one that does, who can give them the up-look.
    Do you know I have a family, where the mother is so ignorant that she cannot tell the time well enough to give

the baby its medicine? The baby is better now, but I would write a note as if to somebody and state the hours the medicine should be given and trust to some of the neighbors happening in. The mother is only twenty and has three children, two are boys, bright too. I cannot hope to do much with the mother, but for the children's sake I keep after her. She is trying, but it is such hard work to see so many things to do. She has not the brain power to grasp it. She has come from a home where she was taught nothing and her mother seems jealous of what is being done for her. It is hard to believe. She is improving some as I keep right on her heels, but when I stop for a while she lets up and lapses. She bemoans her own short comings and is ambitious that her children shall not grow up as ignorant as she has and wants them to be educated.

Talk about city slums! They can't come up to the country slums, more deplorable because of the fresh air and green fields, but it is the isolation, no one seems to know, and no one seems to care very much. I did not intend to write all this, for this woman could not read if she had the book. I've tried to teach her that too. But there are those who could, and would be glad to have it. Thanking you in advance, I am very truly.

Mrs. H.S., Mississippi (July 7, 1916)
Dear Friend:

Before me is your letter of March 14 in which you told me Mrs. H. had requested you sending me copies of Parental Care and Infant Care. About the first of the year we moved here from [another town in Mississippi], and your letter and the Bulletins followed me. I gave them to a

neighbor who feels they were quite a help to her. At Miss
P.'s suggestion I am writing you to put me on your list
changing my address.

   We have no county agent, and, as I am intensely
interested in the Extension work and also Child
Betterment, I ask you to send me copies as you can. I will
distribute them where I think they will do some good.
There is a practice here among Mothers, giving the little
baby catnip tea until five or six weeks old. I asked two of
them why they gave it to the baby. Their answers were,
"Mother gave it to her children" & "I am giving it to
mine," also, "It makes good babies, it makes them sleep."
Now is it possible that catnip tea acts as an opiate? Or
does it not? Would not a little warm water be better if the
baby had colic? I never saw it given before. My boys did
not have it I know.

   A young lady (a school teacher) of this neighborhood
and I are trying to organize the young girls (16 in number)
in to a country club and do what we can along Betterment
lines. We will then be ready for the canning club work
next spring. Thanking you for the Bulletins received and
any favor shown in the future. I am yours truly.

Mrs. W.J., California (June 6, 1917)
My dear Miss Lathrop
   We have a small daughter almost four weeks old
whom we have named K. after our niece. If the Children's
Bureau has made any study of mother's milk and the diet
necessary for needed changes may I have the results? Mine
is far below in fats so that I gain a great deal and K very
little.

   I do so wish more could be done these days to make
human conservation equal to human destruction. Red

Cross Work seems so popular that it makes all of us who
care most for the children long to have them take up
the child welfare, beginning with the conservation of
motherhood. It is a pity the amount spent for war is not
going into something constructive for human welfare.
Very cordially yours.
     P.S. May one of each of your bulletins be sent me? I
will put them where the public can use them.

Mrs. E.M., Missouri (June 22, 1917)
Miss Lathrop,
     I am returning these blanks with much regret. We did
not observe Baby Week here. I know you are a busy
woman, but I hope your secy. may have time to read this
sad, sad letter.
     We live in a saw mill town, better known as a lumber
camp. My husband is manager of the saw mill and I try to
help these poor unfortunate mothers with their babies, but
we have no organized association or club of any kind, and
I am handicapped for doing personal work, expecting a
little one in our home soon.
     A father took his seven months old baby to a physician.
On his return home, the baby died on the train. Of course
people asked the father what was the matter with the
baby. "The doctor gave me some medicine to give it, and
said it was suffering from *neglect*. What is that?" This
actually happ[en]ed. Wasn't it a blessing the poor little
thing died! What a pity such a class of people are parents.
My heart aches for these poor people. Most of the mothers
can not read. I am trying to get a visiting nurse here.
Hope to have a good report next year.
     *Lathrop replies that she has read Mrs. E.M.'s letter "with
very great interest" and "earnestly" hopes that she was suc-*

*cessful in securing a visiting nurse. She asks about the nationality
of the people in the lumber camp, particularly the race and oc-
cupation of the father of the sick baby.*

Mrs. E.M. (July 15, 1917)
Miss Lathrop,

I know what a busy woman you are and I'm enclosing
your letter so you may know the connection.

The father of the baby who died from neglect is an
American; a timber cutter. This baby who died was his
fourth child. The other three are still living. The mother
is living. There are no foreigners in our lumber camp, all
natives of Southeast Missouri. From your map you will see
we live in a new reclaimed district known as ———. Very
few parents in this section can read or write. My heart
aches for the poor children. We can do little for the
parents, *but we must help the children.* Couples marry so
young among this class of people. Girls fifteen and
sixteen, boys eighteen and twenty. This particular case we
speak of, the father had four children and he [is] only
twenty five. I do not know the mother's age. The young
mothers know absolutely nothing about the proper care of
their babies. I have lived here five years, have tried three
different times to organize a mother's club. I keep an
emergency medicine chest and prescribe for sick babies in
ordinary cases. Sore eyes and mouth exist among most of
the babies. Neglect causes that. I keep many bottles of
boric acid solution to give out.

For many years I was a primary teacher and I am deeply
interested in children. We have a boy three years old who
is a perfect specimen of health. His condition gives me a
little prestige and the young mothers seem inclined to take

my advice some times. I'm careful and never give advice unless I'm sure. We are expecting a nurse next week to come, investigate and make us a price for her services. As soon as there is anything to report, rest assured I will.

So much immorality exist[s] among this mill class, young girls are forced to marry so early. Mothers with large families are immoral, no wonder their young daughters go wrong.

I thank you for your time and attention. [The] Lumber Co. works about fifty-five or sixty men. The people who live in the swamps are the same class. Will you be kind enough to send me bulletins suitable for home care of babies that I may look over them and pass on to the few mothers who can read? I had several copies of "Prenatal Care by Mrs. West" I passed on, and they did so much good.

We have a large school attendance, two teachers here. You might put them on your files and send literature. Yours for child welfare.

Our Government
Ought to Protect Us

Despite their different circumstances, both married and widowed women found it necessary to seek financial help from the government. Some married women could not support their families because their husbands could or would not provide for them, and even middle-class women, like Mrs. J.S., might face poverty and lose custody of their children upon divorce or the death of their husbands. Although married women had to rely on private charity, some widows were eligible for state aid. The first mothers' pension law was passed in 1911; by 1919, thirty-nine states had similar laws. In 1935, mothers' pensions were incorporated into the Social Security Act as Aid to Dependent Children. Initially designed to keep children from being removed to asylums because their mothers could not support them, mothers' pensions were considered to be compensation for mothers who raised the nation's citizens. However, by the late 1910s, they had already become identified as charity.[5] Aid was available only for "deserving" mothers who agreed to supervision by the authorities. As these letters indicate, many needy women were ineligible for aid or found it inadequate to meet their needs.

Mrs. H.B., Illinois (February 28, 1916)
Sirs:

After reading your editorial in the paper Daily News entitled Save the babies, I cant help but sit down and write you. I wonder how many of you Gentlemen have ever stopped to consider the cause of infants deaths and why most mothers do not nurse their babies.

5 years ago, 13 Nov, I gave birth to a baby boy. After having been obliged to go without food myself so my other

5. See Edna Bullock, ed., *Selected Articles on Mothers' Pensions* (New York: H.W. Wilson Co., 1915). See also Children's Bureau, U.S. Department of Labor, *Laws Relating to Mothers' Pensions in the United States, Canada, Denmark, and New Zealand*, Dependent Children Series No. 1, Publication No. 7 (Washington, D.C.: Government Printing Office, 1919).

2 little girls could have enough to eat and not go hungry, then my baby was born. And there I was, no food for me, only what was given to me by kind neighbors. The 4th day after birth I had to get up of my sick [bed] and then [on the] tenth day [I] went out to look for work, obtained it, [and] went to work on the 11th day.

I nursed my baby mornings and night, at night time after working all day then nursing my child. Every drop it s[w]ollowed it would throw up. At the same [time] I [was] suffering the awfull torture with my milk, pumping it and throwing it into the sink, while my *baby starved* and my husband *refused* to *provide* for us. At the end of one month my milk had dried up. There [I] was without the fountain nature had provided me with to feed my child. After Christmas, the loss of my position [made me] now unable to buy food for the baby, I must starve and also see the rest of the children do the same. At the end of 3 months my chubby little fellow that weighed 11 lbs at birth now was just merely a skeleton. When the nurse from the welfare Ass. was sent to me [she] asked me to bring the baby to the conference which I did. I exsplained the case and they were kind enough to ask the united Charities to supply me with 1 Pt. of certified [milk]. And following the instructions and [this] help I have raised my boy. He will be 5 years old next Nov. This is only one reason why mothers cant nurse their babies.

Now. Sirs, I am to become a mother again this coming month, and just what I have endured I must go through again. No food for the ones I already have, and nothing to nourish the coming. Only *abuse* and *torture* at the hands of the man who *promised to provide and protect woman.* And *no law to enforce this promise.*

Now, your advice as to regards of clothing. God forbid the mother who wont properly cloth[e] her baby if she can afford it. Mine coming would be without any clothing if the United Charities did not furnish me with a baby layette. Thats is the reason for not [having] proper clothing: We mothers can't afford to buy cloths. Yet each one who sees us will say *why* do you have *children* for such a *man*. Dear Sirs we cant help ourselves. As the saying goes, any fool can have them but it takes a wise one to keep from it; and the law has given man that right. What can us mothers do? Nothing. Only suffer and suffer. With no hand outstretch[ed] to help us. . . . Dirt and dust, how many mothers as well as myself cant afford soap to help clean with? And then Prenatal care during Pregnancy. My god all that I have had to suffer and endure these eight months. No dog need suffer as I have.

I love my children and willing would have as many as possible but never before have I dreaded the ordeal of child birth, as I am afraid to look upon its little face. How can it be human and a perfect child after all that I have been through this last time? Each place I have asked for advice what to do, or for to compel my husband to work and provide for me and the children, the best I receive is, "why do you live with him and have children for such a man? You deserve no pity." Nice advice to poor mothers, who are nothing but fools for men but to bear their children for them, and then afterwards neglect them to go out to work for to buy their food.

God help the poor mothers of today. The cry is Save the babies, but what about the mothers who produce these babies? Now, Dear Sirs, No hard feelling for what I have written. But would it not be better to enact a law that,

when a man marries a woman and she bears his children
for him, that he be compelled to provide for the babies he
caused to be brought into the world, and permit mothers
to properly care for their babies, and give [a man] a life
sentence for bringing home disease and inflicting his wife
with it. And if possible start an association to protect
mothers who are to give birth and after that help them to
help themselves, and enable them to do for their babies.
The Soldier receive his pension, What do mothers'
receive? Abuse, torture, slurs, that is the best they
receive. Men in long service receive their pension.
Mothers deserving receiv[e] nothing.

Now I hope some evening to pick up a newspaper and
be able to read that your department, that you will punish
men so severely who neglect their wife and children that
their will be less need of advice to *mothers*. Only I beg of
you to do something to protect mothers in the pitfall I find
myself in. When my baby is born, will I be able to feed it?
Or will I be compelled again to leave my infant and work,
for to buy for the other 3 as well as the new one—and
have to pay some one else to look after the little one I
love to put to my breast and let it grow and live? Or will it
mean starvation again as before? The time is drawing
near, but I would sooner go through the fires of H than
the misery I have had to go through.

Now please excuse me for writing this to your dept. but
I just could not help doing so. You may send me all the
reading matter you have on prenatal care, and infant care.
It may give me a little encouragement. So thanking you
many times for reading this, and [I hope] that through
your help all mothers the same as myself will get some
consideration.

I also have a little girl 8 years old who is frail, and the school doctor tells her to eat fresh eggs and drink fresh milk and lots of it, but where am I to get it? I can see her going into decline right along, but what am I to do? Think it over gentlemen. Se[e] if you cant make men do a little different, and then there will be better babies, better mothers, better grown children, and a better country, and less human beings in the penaten[t]ierey.

I trust you will look at this in the right light and excuse for crying out my soul to you. Sincerely yours.

Please do not use my name in publication as the children would be jeered at by the neighbors children.

Lathrop writes Mrs. H.B. that she "realize[s] the importance of all you say" and then writes to Alice Hamilton at Hull House to ask whether she "or someone equally noninstitutional" would call on her. She also asks about publishing parts of Mrs. H.B.'s letter.

Mrs. H.B. (March 20, 1916)
My dear Miss Lathrop:

Received your letter and must thank you for your kind words therein. Allso for the books. I have read them and they are indeed very interesting to me. The Friend you said would call on me, I had the pleasure of meeting her Sunday March 19, and found her to be a most pleasing and lovable person—so different from the other people I have met. And Miss Lathrop you ask permission to use my letter. You may do so and I am only sorry that I cant be of some service to you. I am still on my feet but expect to be confined any day now. I did not get the lady's name who called on me. I was so taken up with her I forgot to ask

her. Now with my best wishes for your work. I remain
yours truly.
     P.S. I trust you will forgive me for some of things I said
in my other letters.

Mrs. G.H., North Carolina (October 5, 1917)
     I read your notice "Protect the Children" in the
Ladies Home Journal. I am very much in need of your
advice. I hardly know how to state my trouble but will try
to do it in as few words as possible. I am an invalid and
kept ill all the time through my husbands ill treatment
and management. He does not allow me to have one word
to say about anything but always blames me for everything
that happens. He will not allow me to sleep any where in
the house, only on a cot where the colored cook used to
sleep (when he would keep one), or in the dining room on
the floor. He will not provide for me in any way, only that
I share the food, shelter and fuel with the children. I
cannot stand it to sleep where he forces me to, for it is
to[o] cold and I am disturbed so much about sleep.
     My husband will not do anything for me that might
benefit my health nor allow me to do anything for myself,
even things that don't cost a cent. He [started] when I got
to[o] weak to work . . . just after an operation, when the
doctor said I must do no work for a year, and only let me
leave the hospital with the understanding that I need not
work. My husband has threatened to kill me, but I jumped
out of the window and ran to one of the neighbors. Only
the other day he said right before the children that He
and they ought to kill me. He just keeps me ill all the
time. There is always something, like at present I must

sleep in the place prepared for the colored cook. I could sleep so much better if I could sleep away from the noise; besides, it is already to[o] cold for me, and I have a sore throat and pains in my chest and lungs, as my vitality has been kept so low for so long.

Though this man get about twelve dollars per day he will not hire any help in the house, nor will he let me. The strain got so hard on me the other day that, as I have 12 dollars left of some money my father left me, I thought I would risk $6 for a cook for two weeks, but my husband wouldn't allow it. I am an invalid at present unable to get food even for my self, though when troubles and worry let up a little and conditions are better for a little while, I always gain right along. But just as soon as my husband sees I am gaining he always does something to make circumstances to[o] much for me. He declares I am perfectly well and strong, and won't even allow me to go to a physician who makes a specialty of such cases as mine and gives free consultation and xray examination. He also declares he will see I die before he does and says I am insane.

He has forced me to use over eight hundred dollars of my own money for the family, and last winter borrowed $150 of me (I had to let him have it) and promised to pay it any time I needed it—but won't let me have a cent of it. Because last summer when there was so many vegetables and melons and tomatoes [that] we could not use all he brought from the farm, this fall he wouldn't buy any seeds for the garden at all. He would buy nothing but roses. They make winter garden here, and as the garden would be made on the farm it wouldn't cost him an extra cent, only for the seed. But he would buy nothing but roses. Just think, with everything so high and nothing much to get here!

I have three children, a boy 13, but he is so small and nervous, [and] two girls, 14 and 15. The health of the eldest is in bad condition. I wrote to Dr. Kellog of Battle Creek, Mich. . . . and he said if this girl had to work now she never would be able to work at all. With the over work and worry, the other girl is fast getting in the same condition. When I told my husband what the doctor said, he said he wasn't going to listen and I had just got to stop writting to old grandmothers. These children are all trying their best to get an education but they can do nothing this way, [with] ill health and no one to cook any thing. The weight of it all is to[o] much for them. I have prayed and studdied to know how to take care of my children, but my husband won't let me do a thing.

It is bad enough for a mother to have her children crying hungry when the father is poor, but when he rides in an Overland, has a farm and earns about 12 dollars per day, its to[o] much. He is forcing them to do what he could hire done for 50 cents a day. . . . It would make a well woman ill to try to get along, say nothing about three children who are ill and trying to keep up in school. Oh, it is terrible to try to get along where there is no mother to do or keep track of a thing. My husband reads nothing, studdies nothing, only making towels, [but] thinks he knows it all and is always afraid we will forget he is boss. He is scarce ever at home, goes to [town] Saturday and Sunday. When he says a thing is so it must be so and when he says a thing must be done so, it must. And its no use to tell him the results, for he will listen to nothing. The children are afraid of him and dare not let him know

they are ill if they can [possibly] get out of bed. The eldest
girl was ill a few days and he called her lazy and said she
would rather lay around than stir. If the health of the girls
is not attended to now it never can be right . . . .

My husband says every thing he does is right and he
will never learn anything, for he always blames me for
everything. He says if it hadn't been for me, he would
have had thousands of dollars, and seems to hold a hatred
towards me about it. I know he hasn't spent 10 dollars on
me in two years. I have tried to tell you the conditions so
you will be able to judge if there is any chance for me and
my children.

I was raised on a farm and am willing and anxious to
work. All of my children are anxious to get along and love
to work garden and care for chicken and animals. I
understand fully about the care of hens and chickens and
pigs and know quite a lot about gardening. And there is
such a good chance on my husband's farm to raise flowers
and vegetables and poultry for [town]. It is only 17 miles
from [town]. I wonder if it would be possible to get any of
my money back so I could get treatment and rent a little
place of my own. I understand about marketing things and
have studdied up the plans for making up a line of relishes
for the market, but I must have some degree of health
before I can do anything. Now, I ask you to tell me if
there is any chance for me and my children. For certainly
unless something is done soon we shall all be helpless
soon. I am getting so much fever, and I am sure the winter
will prove to[o] much for me, with no one to cook or keep
the house warm, and trying to get a long with three
children ill, and trying to do on nothing. They haven't
even sufficient clothing or school books.

Just now my husband has come in to his dinner. The

children have been home from school but ten minutes. He is scolding because they haven't their aprons on, though he will buy none and they must use towels. One child says she had to hurry so because mother wasn't able to start dinner to day and he says "she is just as able as any body, don't believe any of that kind of nonsense." For one thing, I have a floating kidney and if I get around much it makes me so ill I cannot bare it. I have tried to be a Christian and live each day so I would not have to look back on it with regret. And I cannot believe God will desert my children and my self now. My husband forced me to work so far and force my nerves to such a terrible length that they are in a terrible state. . . . Doctors have said what I needed, but my husband declares no one ever found anything wrong with me and I am perfectly well. I cannot tell him the children are hungry (we can [get] about what we want at the store, but there isn't much there; besides, it needs to be prepared and put on the table properly, and the children, being as they are, haven't natural abilities any way), or [that] the work is to[o] much, for he won't listen to anything. There are so many things to think of to keep a house going. Only those who have tried it know how everything is against us. All I can do for my country is to raise three children so that the world may be better for their having been in it, but if I don't have help they will only be drags to the world. Thanking you for you[r] kind interest in advance.

Lathrop writes, "You will understand that I am not writing to you now officially but just as one person to another. Sometimes it does work miracles if a man who has been all his life accustomed to his own way is suddenly shown that the law and public opinion have another way, and I can not but think that it might be true with your husband. Perhaps your gentleness and yieldingness have blinded him to the fact that the law itself, as you could ascertain by consulting a man like the Mayor of your town, is against him. The law about families is intended to protect children, and children can not be protected and given the peace and quiet which they need for healthful growing up unless there is a good understanding between the father and mother. I wish I knew of some way to be of service to you."

Mrs. W.P., California (May 20, 1918)

I am writing to ask if there is any law in this Bureau that will help me to locate and make my husband support myself and two children, a girl aged 10 and Boy 11 yrs: he deserted his family last Aug. We have not had any support from him for several months. I think he is in Cleveland Ohio or Detroit Mich. or in that part of the Country. He is a man capable of earning a good salary, say $200.00 per month. And with the high cost of living I am not able to earn enough to properly support the children. They are being under fed and neglected in many ways. It seems to me that our Government ought to have some way of protecting us in such cases as this when women or men deliberately set about to wreck a home and leave helpless children to starve to death or happen to them what will.

It seems that the Authority of one state does not reach into another state, and it seems to[o] bad for when the verry future of our glorious Cou[n]try depends on the children of today for it[s] future men & women. They must be well trained, [and] so much or all of that depends chiefly on the home. Hoping that you can be of some assistance to me. I am verry sincerely.

Emma Lundberg refers Mrs. W.P. to the proper agency and tells her that "there is throughout the country cooperation of

agencies in various cities who assist each other in just such cases
and we feel sure that your local organization can help you get
justice and secure support for your children."

Mrs. G.A., Pennsylvania (April 13, 1927)

   I am writing you concerning my children support. My
husband died last fall leaveing me with 3 little boys and I
am not able to work to support them as I am expecting to
take my bed any day now.

   So I wanted to see if I could get this mothers Pension as
I am in bad means with these Children, as I have been
trying to keep them together and hate so much to part
them, but will hafto do some thing with them pretty soon
if I dont get help from some wheres pretty soon.

   So please Answer and tell me if I could get this pension
for these childrens support.

Mrs. J.S., Illinois (May 9, 1927)

   Will you please send me information about the
Mother's pension law? I was left a widow last April 1926,
and have been told I am not entitled to this fund because
I own our home. I have five children, the oldest only
fourteen years of age, the youngest four. I have a little
store (groceries), but the neighborhood is not built up
enough to make it pay and I cannot leave home to take up
outside work. I am not strong enough to do very heavy
work.

   I am in rather desperate straits. Four children are in
school and the clothing is quite an item. By keeping this
little grocery I am enabled to get my own groceries at cost,
but I cannot feed & clothe and keep up household

expenses with out help. The oldest boy has a Sunday
paper route, but only makes about one dollar fifty cents a
sunday. So I will appreciate any information, as I do want
to keep my children with me. Respectfully.

Mrs. S.W., Miami, Florida (May 19, 1927)
Dear Mrs.

I wants to [k]now about this instruction, for my self
in Family way an[d] i is not able to Bear no Big Exspences.
An[d] i am glad to have a Part in the Boa[r]d of He[a]lth.
In my Condiacon, could i Be taken Care of in the Boa[r]d
of He[a]lth? I only have 3 monthes to go an[d] i have to
work hard For a liveing. I am a widow. The man that got
me this way, he Promes to take Care of me an[d] said he
would marry me. But he fail to do so an[d] I want a word
From. I am the mother of 9, 5 liveing. An[d] Please send
me [or] write me what to do about it an[d] give me
information. I would Be glad to here, so i can go down to
the Board of He[a]lth. So I will close. Return to Miami
Fla.

Mrs. M.S., Minnesota (August 20, 1927)
Sir's

I am sending two letters to you which I received in
my effort to get the Mothers pension for my two minor
children, age 12, and 14, and all the support I have is my
washings. And [I] had to have county support when my
children was down with scarlet fever and we were
quarantined, and could not take in washing. And twice
two of my Children was operated on for appendicitis. Am
washing for the Doctor now to pay for the bill and was

down sick one winter. So I had to have helps. Other mothers get's there mothers pensions that is no more deserving of it than I and it will do away with this County alms. I tried to get it the last three years, and when I try to find out about it, they tell me my boy's can work. One boy 17, is in high school, and K. is 19 and wants to work his way through college, and I do want my children to be educated. It is all I can give them. My husband has been gone six years and the 1st year he sent me some money, but not over $100.00 in all. I am divorsed from him. They gave men helps from this town with family. Why cant a mother alone get it without it being used as a weapon to keep her from her Mothers pension that every singel mother with minor children is entitled to. Respt.

Mrs. M. S. *enclosed a letter she had received from the local agency administering mothers' pensions, which stated that since she had already received $959.72 in four years, she was not entitled to any more aid. Agnes Hanna of the Children's Bureau replies that there is nothing the federal agency can do.*

I Suffered Hell
on Earth because of
a Doctor

In the 1910s, the Children's Bureau staff corresponded with a number of women who lived too far away from doctors to obtain medical care. However, by the 1920s, medical care was more widely available, and the Bureau received numerous letters complaining about doctors. Although many women had expected that physician-attended hospital births would remove the dangers of childbirth, their letters show that medical care was not necessarily safer. Some women were permanently injured and others lost children because of incompetent or overzealous physicians and the increase in instrumental deliveries. Women accused physicians of insensitivity, carelessness, and greed. They worried because they had no control over doctors and asked the Children's Bureau to warn other women about them. Two of the letters are from women concerned about the wisdom of the medical advice they received concerning circumcision.

Mrs. W.M., Virginia (March 29, 1915)
Dear Miss Lathrop

I am writing to you to know more about the birth registration. I can not find anyone here that can tell me. I expected to have a Dr when my baby was born, and he was sent for, but had gone to the Court House, fifteen miles away. Then a midwife was sent for, but did not come in time, so there was only a neighbor present to wait on me. The midwife does not understand about birth registration, only knew there was such, but I did not know any more than at first.

Back here in the country we Mothers are expected to get on alright any way. . . . My babys eyes have been sore but no one worried but myself, and I did only because I had read of the danger of blindness in your books.[6] It can

6. To prevent ophthalmia neonatorum, a common form of blindness caused by an eye infection at birth, *Prenatal Care* advised that a physician or nurse put drops of silver nitrate into a newborn baby's eyes.

open them this morning, and I have tried to be as careful as I could with them. No one here ever saw a Dr. do any thing for a newborn baby's eyes.

I have a young expectant Mother's name to send in to you. I want the books sent to her, altho she has just gone to the city to live. Very truly.

Mrs. H.A., Wyoming (July 2, 1918)

Dear Sir:

I am a young mother with a three week old son. A bottle baby. I am going to live in a new oil field twenty six miles from a Doctor, five miles from a telephone and a quarter of a mile from my nearest neighbor.

I wish you would kindly send me all the information possible about feeding and careing for my baby. I am enclosing a self-addressed envelope and two three cent stamps. Thanking you in advance for information, I remain.

Mrs. A.T., Missouri (March 28, 1922)

Just a little over two years ago I wrote to you, and now I am going to write again. Little over 17 months ago I gave Birth to a fine Baby boy. He was very Large and I am all toren from the Birth of that child and the Doctor I had never even examined me to see if I was all right. And now I suffer day and night. I just suffer that I dont care for nothing and I want to know by the Law what I can do to that doctor for not taking care of me when birth of the Baby. I just feel like my life is ruined since I gave birth to my second child. I dont feel able to do my work. I am just

a [w]reck. I am in such mishery I wish I could have a
midwife to examine me as I hate to go to a doctor. Dr. F.
from ____wa[i]ted on me and I tell my husband that I need
treatment but he dont believe in a doctor. So hear I am. I
remain.

Mrs. R.P., Iowa (February 19, 1924)
U.S. Dept of Labor:—
     Will you send your bulletin on Prenatal Care to
[two friends]? They are each of these far advanced in
pregnancy. I cannot say how many months—I should
judge at least seven or more—but I am sure they can glean
some useful information.
     Two years ago this month I was pregnant—as near as I
could tell about 2 1/2 months. A friend gave me one of
your bulletins. It seemed I followed instructions so
carefully, and I felt fine until I became constipated. I took
Senns Tea and Senns Prunes until it made me sick to
attempt to take it—but I took it anyhow, with no relief
whatever. We live so far out from medical aid—and I
simply didn't know what else to take that would not be
harmful. I had planned to go some way to Doctor next
day—which was two whole days no bowel movement. But
the strain and all brought a miscarriage. Or at least I can
think of nothing else which did it. I have never been
pregnant since. Have been married almost nine years and
have only been pregnant the one time. Have had
examinations by the leading doctors and they find nothing
wrong. I am telling you this thinking perhaps you will lay
greater stress upon what to do with such obstinate
constipation.
     If only I might become pregnant again, I believe I could

get thru alright. I am taking Squibbs Mineral Oil which keeps me in fine condition. I always become constipated at my menstruation period unless I take something and suffer untold agony every month. Pardon my relating my personal experience but I tell it only with a motive that you may help somebody else and too that you may give me any more information that you may have.

You speak of patent medicines as being fake. I have always thot so. But I believe Medical doctors drive one to Chiropractors and patent medicines. One goes to them, they make a little examination, charge for it and say, oh, in time you'll probably be alright. And one goes on hoping. And yet if one is clear down in bed with a high temperature these same doctors will go thru storms and bad roads to get to a patient. Thanking you for sending information to the above friends, also for any help you may give me. I am, respectfully yours.

Florence Kraker writes, "Your unfortunate experience is only one of many which the Maternity and Infancy Act is now endeavoring to prevent in the rural sections. [The chief of the Division of Health in] Iowa City now has on his staff a number of obstetricians and pediatricians who are holding prenatal and infant clinics through the State. If you will write to him he will be glad to advise you when they will hold one in your county. They will give you a complete physical examination such as is outlined in the enclosed folder with such personal advice as may be necessary.

"The importance of prenatal care has not until quite recently been fully realized by the medical profession as well as the general public and the subject of preventive medicine is still quite new. That women realize and appreciate the need of prenatal care is a great factor in developing the service rendered."

Mrs. W.I., Michigan (April 15, 1924)
Dear Sirs:—

I am writing you for information. In november I was down to Ann Arbor and had an operation for *something*, anyway they took part of my [innards]. What part I do not know. I went before a *large class* of students, also some Doctors. The Doctors could not all agree. They turned on x-rays, took pictures etc. And when I asked them what was the matter they told me there was *nothing the matter*.

Now some of the people up here know too. They ask me, and when I tell them the Doctors wouldn't tell me, they act so queer. Haven't I just as much a right to know [what happened to me] as my neighbors? I'm the one who had the *Bull-Dog Determination* to see the thing thru. They did not. I'm all most sure I lost [a baby] at the second month and carried one [to term]. It is on record down there. I quicken the 22nd of Febr.

Are we the mothers of the race going to be the goats? Isn't it my right to know what other people know and [I] want to know? Mr. I. said, "This is the first one out of five that you have not *heave* up in your [innards]." They done some thing. Why didn't they want me to know? . . . Did I have a baby and was it crippled or what? And then got that way again? I do not understand why I should not know. I want the truth and nothing but the *whole truth*. No more pacifiers for me please. Hoping this will be confidential and that at last I can get some satisfaction. Look on both sides of the fence. Don't be *narrow-minded*, never blame anyone for what you want to know or do yourself.

We, the laboring class, are as a general rule doing our share in raising up the race and also our *share* of the work. Babies mean work, but it is the kind we like to do, so it

don't matter. I'm very thankful I haven't had such a time
with my stomach, as it has been hard to get help. Some
can not boil water without burning it. And I like to do
the work myself. Enclosed please find a 2 cts. stamp for
reply. Hoping I have found one friend who is sincere and
honest at last. I beg to remain yours truly.

P.S. . . . I'm sending this to Chicago to be mailed. I'm
suspicious of every body for some reason. (They have told
me too many lies.) I will guarantee that no one will ever
find out if you tell me. Please don't let anyone know that I
wrote. *I will not do no more* in helping raise the race unless
I get some satisfaction this time.

*June Hull replies that she can't tell Mrs. W.I. the cause or
nature of her operation or current problems without more information on her condition prior to the operation and a physical examination. Estimating that Mrs. W.I. is in her fifth month of
pregnancy, she advises that "for your own good health and that
of your baby you should cease to worry about what has happened
and conserve all your resources for motherhood in the interest of
your coming baby. I fear you have not realized that the recent
operation, followed so soon by pregnancy, is making a very great
drain on your nervous system, and for this reason you are more
sensitive to the conduct of those about you than you would be
under normal conditions. You should think about it this way, try
to rest more, and in this way you will overlook many things and
be serene, quiet and happy until your baby comes."*

Mrs. M.M., Indiana (March 3, 1926)
To the Childs Bureau Department

You may think this very ignorant of me but as it has
caused me so much worry I would like you [to] explain to
me. I have a baby 18 months old. I was confined at the

Hospital at the time; my Dr. was away on his vacation so I was compelled to select another. I live in the country and was not acquainted with any of the City Dr. but selected one as I knew through others to be one of the leading Dr. He told me my baby needed to be circumcised and that then was the time to have it done. I was ignorant of anything of the kind, had never saw anything of the kind, but as the nurses told me it was best, I left it to them. They told me it did not hurt them much and only took a few days to be well, but it hurt him so badly he cried and scratched his face and his lips looked as if they were ready to bleed. The nurse told me he took five stitches, a lap stitch underneath, as it bled more than [the doctor] liked. My baby did not grow for weeks and cried. [It] was at least three weeks before it was perfectly healed and [it was] swol[l]en for five or six. He gave what he called complete circumcision. The skin is cut back so far. Do you think this was done properly? It does not cause any trouble now, but the baby pulls at himself so much and at times it gets as red as blood. Do you think it will ever cause any trouble or is it natur[a]l for this to be red; it looks so bad. I have been unable to find any literature on this. I know there were several others circumcised at the Hospital but none cried like my baby. Why would Dr.s urge anything of the kind?

Another Dr. has told me since that it is not neccessary, that the skin could be stretched, but he has never saw my baby. Please explain this to me as it has caused me so much worry. Please send me the book pre-Natal care—5c. Thanking you, I remain.

Anderson responds that circumcision should be done at an early age and is often necessary, "as it was in your baby's case."

She assures Mrs. M.M. that stitches and "considerable irritation" are common, "even under the best conditions." "Most babies pull at themselves so that this means very little except that it is well not to leave the baby uncovered too much. Also it is best not to take the baby's hand away or [in] any way call his attention to the act. A baby very soon learns to make an association between an act and a feeling, and we do not wish a baby to know that he is doing anything objectionable in pulling at himself.

"Probably the best thing for you to do is to put the matter out of your mind as something that needed to be done, has been done and done well, and that it is done and over with. Unquestionably this is the best thing for your baby."

Mrs. P.O., Iowa (July 23, 1928)
Dear Mrs. Abbott,

The government books which I obtained from your department have been of such wonderful help to me in raising my three lovely children that two friends of mine would like a copy of them also. Will you kindly send a copy of "Infant Care," "Child Care," "Child Management" and "Prenatal Care" [to them]?

There is one thing on which I would like a little advise, which has been omitted from your children books and all others which I have read. Do you think all or nearly all baby boys should be circumcised? My baby boy, now three months old was born at the local hospital, and while I was yet on the delivery table the doctor said that on the eighth day he ought to be circumcised. I was taken home the 4th day and my mother-in-law, a mid-wife, and my husband objected to circumcision and it was not done.

My mother-in-law insisted that she had taken care of

scores of babies that had never been circumcised and said that if I kept pushing back the foreskin and always kept it clean under the foreskin, with washing and occasional application of vasaline that that was all that was necessary. My husband agreed with her.

Now a friend of mine, a teacher, informs me that I was foolish to have listened to their advise and that all professors, psyc[h]ologists, teachers, nurses and doctors advocate circumcision. She said that unless it was performed they were more apt to be mentally dumb.

What is your advise or that of Mrs. Max West? I am a good mother and want to do what is right in all respects. One objection my husband had was that two cases he knew of the doctors cut the foreskin too short leaving the tender part exposed causing much distress to the child.

I am greatly worried about the situation as I want to do what is best for the future boy and man. A little light on the subject and a little unbiased advice would be like removing millstones from my neck. Thanking you in advance, yours sincerely. P.S. I have no one else to whom I could go for advice.

Frances Hennessy tells Mrs. P.O. that decisions regarding circumcision should rest with the doctor. She says she knows nothing about a child's being mentally dumb if not circumcised and urges Mrs. P.O. to write the state university research division on maternity and infancy hygiene.

Mrs. E.H., Michigan (received January 9, 1931)
Dear Miss Abbott:

I tuned in this morning as the child's health program was coming to a close. I wonder if I may suggest to you, in

your talks, if you would explain to the mothers or mothers
to be just what they might demand in the line of care
before baby comes.

I write to you because a few months ago I lost my first
born, and I believe if I had received proper care my child
would have lived. My doctor was a very clever man, and I
had every faith in him: at three months, I made my first
visit to him. I had blood pressure taken and urine test; he
told me at six months he would put me on a diet to keep
the baby from getting large. At six months he said I did
not need to go on diet as the baby was small. I knew the
baby was going to be large and I asked several times about
the diet, but still he said no. I ate only things I knew
would be good for baby and myself: fruits and vegetables,
no meat, tea or coffee. I was never weighed once, no
measurements were taken, and I gained over forty pounds.
But still I figured he knew his business more than I did so I
never said any more.

A month before my baby was born I took a few pains,
and I had a trembling feeling for a few hours. I went to see
my doctor and he said he wouldn't be surprised if I had
started in labor and the baby may be born that night or
the next day, though my pains had stopped and I was told
to go home and take a dose of castor oil. I did that but
nothing happened. I was quite sick all the way through;
his medicine never had any affect on me. Two weeks
before child birth he told me to take some more castor oil,
and said if the child was born that month, it would be a
small baby.

I went to the hospital and I couldn't explain my pain
those last two hours. I thought I would go out of my mind:
I was left all alone in a small room, and the nurses closed

the door so they could not hear me scream. The next thing, twelve hours after I entered the hospital my doctor walked in, and said we are going to take it. My baby was born feet first and weighed ten pounds. I was under ether four and one half hours. They told me the next day my childs heart beat for an hour but they could not get him to breathe. I would appreciate a reply to this letter and I thank you. Yours truly.

Blanche Haines sends Mrs. E.H. a copy of Prenatal Care, *which includes information on what to "expect and demand" during pregnancy. "Of course you understand it is very much easier to get it from a book than it would be to talk over these very intimate things on the radio." She stresses the importance of physical examinations, blood pressure readings, urinalyses, moderate weight gain, and measuring the bones of the pelvis for women with a first baby. "A 10 pound baby is a big baby and probably accounts for the fact that you had to have it taken and it resulted disastrously," she concludes. "I hope you will have better luck next time and this will help you to know what you should have done."*

Mrs. R.C., Florida (January 27, 1932)
Dear Madam,

This letter may appear presumptuous and my suggestions superfluous. Nevertheless I am anxious to tell you of my experience in the hope that it may lead to your giving additional advice as regards labor and medical attention during that time.

My child was born July 6, 1931, two weeks after my 27th birthday, and although I had always been a healthy normal young woman previous to that time, I have been an invalid since—the direct result of neglect in one of Cincinnati's (Ohio) largest maternity hospitals and at the hands of a supposedly ranking obstetrician.

Early in pregnancy, I wrote to the Department of Labor and received your booklet on Prenatal Care. I note that you say it is usually not necessary for the doctor to remain with the patient during the first stage of labor. I feel that if there had been some statement as to when or how long after pains had begun the doctor should give the patient an examination to determine progress, I might have been prepared to cope with the situation which arose.

Then, too, there is an unfortunate condition in the hospitals in Cincinnati, and, from conversations with women and nurses in various parts of the country, I believe it exists in many places. The nurses are so intimidated by the doctors that they are afraid to call them for a woman in labor for fear the doctor will say it is too soon and jeer and rebuke them. They prefer to let the patient suffer. The nurses admitted this to me afterwards. Another graduate nurse of the same hospital named a doctor in Cincinnati who will not permit that he be called sooner than an hour before delivery. Who can judge to such a nicety?

Many women have told me that doctors and nurses take advantage of a woman who is having her first child and do not give her the proper attention because she does not know enough to require it. A graduate nurse made the same statement to me.

I phoned my doctor that I was having labor pains ten minutes apart. He told me to go to the hospital, that they would call him when my pain became severe, and that he would see me when he made his morning calls. I phoned

him at 1 am. He came at 9 am and my child was born at
9:57, an instrumental delivery. In the interim I received
little or no attention, was left alone in the room with my
door closed, suffered unspeakable and indescribable agony,
sustained a strained and enlarged heart with a leaking
valve because of the ordeal, and, later, and at present, a
nervous breakdown.

It seems to me that eight hours is too long to leave a
woman without a medical examination. I have talked with
many women who tell of similar experiences, one in
Philadelphia, another in Chicago, another in New York,
etc. Do you not think it would be a safeguard if a woman
were advised to have an agreement with her doctor that
he is to come when her husband calls him and remain
with her until the child is born? So many women have
told me of the doctor's coming and then leaving with the
assurance that the nurses will call him, well knowing that
they will not dare to waste his time by calling too soon or
soon enough!

Contrary to the attitude that statistics show most
college graduates hold, my husband and I felt that we
wanted to have children. After this experience we are firm
advocates of birth control and our friends feel that our
experience is one by which they can profit. This may
doubtless seem a ridiculous statement, but I know of a
surprising number of young married couples who are
appalled by my experience. Very truly yours.

P.S. I am spending the winter in Florida trying to
become able to care for my baby, who is in the north with
my husband. I state this to explain my location and the
foregoing statements.

*Haines responds that they will consider Mrs. R.C.'s com-
ments when revising* Prenatal Care, *although circumstances*

make each case different. "*I am sorry that you had such an unfortunate time, and I do hope you are improving. I do not feel that all women have had the experience you had. An institution necessarily has a much more impersonal attitude towards patients than a private physician and private nurse would have.*"

Mrs. A.E., Minnesota (August 10, 1932)
Dear Sirs:

About six years ago I made the acquaintance of govt publications Infant Care, Prenatal Care etc. This book Infant Care did me more good than the Dr. I had at the time my baby was born. I did not have a great deal of money and the information in these booklets was [concise] and helpful. I just felt that I should write and tell you how grateful I was that one can get even this little bit of free advice from our govt. We should be able to get more medical help and advice from our gov't regarding babies and child raising.

Our Gov't should have a check on doctors. We should be able to write to the Dept. of Labor and get a list of certified doctors who are capable and sincere about handling child birth. I feel that I should write of my experience. In these publications the advice is consult a reputable or family physician. I should like to ask you how one knows who *is* a reputable physician? What check other than public opinion is there on a doctor who is not reputable? Do you realize that doctors are so well organized and the profession has such ethics between themselves that it is almost impossible to check a doctor for malpractice? It requires money and is very hard to prove, so that medical men do about as they please. Is this the way it should be?

I was cared for when my son was born by Dr. B. He is supposed to be a reputable surgeon and qualified for maternity work. I was in the hospital two weeks at the time of his birth. I placed myself under his care about several months before he was born. He never advised a change of diet but I went from 110 lbs to 158 lbs the year he was born. I had a very hard birth, was torn and had three stitches, two surface and one deep tore the floor of the womb. When I left the hospital, Miss L., his head nurse, removed the stitches after they had been in two weeks. Then I went home. Dr. B. did not tell me to come back for further examination later but just let me go. I had milk fever while in the hospital and breast trouble. Then after I got home I was in bed for about two weeks with milk fever. Nothing was done about this.

My baby had colic and green bowels and loose bowels for about a year [and] cried a great deal of the time night and day, necessitating [us] moving because of his crying. The doctor did not advise a change of food for him and I thought often he would die from this. I nursed him until he was thirteen months.

He had scarlet fever when he was eleven months old. It was in the treatment of this that your books on baby care [came] in handy. I followed advice given in Infant Care and he came out of it well and without any complications. He cut all of his teeth by the time he was 13 mon. This Dr. advised me that my baby had heat rash [and] to take off his clothing and make him cooler, over the telephone. I did not follow his advice but became exasperated and called another doctor who pronounced it had scarlet fever.

About two years after my babys birth I did not feel right. I became nervous, the back of my neck and head hurt, and I felt like sitting down all of the time. I went to Dr. B. [and] explained how I felt. He did not give me a thorough examination but quickly pronounced it nervousness and gave me a bromide, which I took for a long time, just covering up my trouble. I broke down completely and went to the hospital again, where no examination was made but a goiter test was given, and I was given iodine all of the time I was there.

Later we moved to St. Paul and a more competent doctor examined me. He said I had not been properly cared for after Child birth and that I was torn. He scraped my womb and took stitches. My health has improved [but] my nervous system is badly shattered. I am sore all through my back and shoulders and the back of my neck. I haven't slept real well for a long time. Now I will never be like I was if I had been properly cared for.

I graduated from a state teachers college and taught successfully four years. I had a very fine record. My son is now healthy and very intelligent, and it is hard for me to bring him up because of this trouble. I would have enjoyed raising him very much if I had stayed well. I came from a family of eight children, was the oldest girl, and helped to raise a family of intelligent brothers and sisters. I worked and saved very hard to get my education. My memory is impaired and my time sense seems to be gone, rendering my accuracy and ability a lot less than it used to be. I am carrying on doing the best that I can.

I want to say again that those government publications were a great consolation and help to me. I have told many about them. When one hasn't much money these things are greatly appreciated.

I have suffered endless torture and unnecessary worry

and pain because of this doctors carelessness or ignorance, I don't know which. Life for me will never be as full. I have no come back on him. This same man had a verdict rendered against him on a malpractice case for bone setting some time ago. Now there seems to be nothing but public opinion to combat such practice. This Dr. B. I believe is in the blue book of surgeons.

Doctors all over our land are performing illegal operations too, and there seems to be no way of checking that. All it takes is ready cash for a woman or girl to relieve herself of the responsibility of a baby. This cheapens motherhood, ruins womanhood and encourages immorality. Operations of all kinds are emphasized because there is money in that, but maternity work is so neglected and a great many doctors know so little about baby raising that any old lady who has raised a family can give you better advice.

I have been wanting to put these facts before some body or organization with power and authority for a long time. I feel it my duty. Kindly read this and use your influence to better conditions in this respect. I think a gov't check on hospitals, doctors and operations is coming some day and it will be a good thing. Often times patients are unnecessarily held in hospitals after having operations for a longer period than necessary just to run up a bill. Every thing is done so underhanded and secretly among doctors and nurses that it is very hard for a patient to get a square deal.

This comes from the heart and soul of one who has suffered hell on earth because of carelessness and neglect by a doctor in the medical profession. I was an intelligent person seeking all the advice and knowledge I could get about babies and baby raising before my baby came. I was very pleased to get these government publications. I would have come out better, but your publications fail to tell how to detect a reputable physician, and I am marred for life because of this. The Gov't should have a list of qualified tried and true maternity doctors that a prospective mother could get by sending for it. This should go along with the publication. Please consider this suggestion. Sincerely yours.

[P.S.] Kindly advise me what I can do in a case like this if there is no help for me. Please use your influence to prevent further ruination of mothers by such practice.

James McCord replies that Mrs. A.E.'s problem is "unfortunately not rare" but that the Bureau cannot publish a list of reputable physicians because licensing is a state matter. "Government participation in maternity and infancy must of necessity be along educational lines rather than any supervision of individual physicians. The ultimate solution of the problem of good obstetrics lies first in the medical schools' turning out men who are well trained in the fundamental principles of the practice of obstetrics, and secondly the education of the women of this country to the appreciation of what good obstetrics really means. One can not work without the other."

I Have Children
So Fast It Is Wrecking
My Life

As a result of the reputation of the Children's Bureau for helping women and because of publicity about the birth-

control movement, the agency began in the 1920s to receive letters inquiring about birth control. The letters came
from the young and the middle aged, from women who had
large families and from those who were childless. Despite
their different circumstances, most women wanted to limit
their families for health reasons or because they had trouble
supporting a family on a limited income; the concept of
choice had not yet appeared. Because birth control was illegal and because conservatives attacked the Sheppard-
Towner Act by accusing its supporters of advocating it, the
Children's Bureau was not legally or politically able to provide women with birth control information. According to
Bureau physician Martha Eliot, Abbott was not opposed to
birth control but thought that advocating it during the
1920s would be a political mistake.[7] Therefore, the Children's Bureau answers to these poignant letters about birth
control stated tersely that they had no information on the
subject or ignored that section of the letter completely.

Mrs. T.M., North Dakota (October 14, 1921)
    The other day I read a letter in a daily paper from a
woman who said parents have no right to bring more
children into the world than they can properly take care
of and educate. I have written to the paper for this woman
to tell what to do so as not to have more than wanted and

7. Martha May Eliot Interview, 420–422, Family Planning Oral History Project, 1973–1976, SL. Eliot implies that Abbott was sympathetic
to birth control, but as late as 1936 Katharine Lenroot (then the Children's Bureau chief) opposed it. On Lenroot's view, see David Kennedy,
Birth Control in America (New Haven, Conn.: Yale University Press,
1970), 260–265.

the paper itself answered for me to write to the Children's Bureau for information. I am the mother of seven and only 22 years old. I did not want any more after I had two. Yours.

Miss L.A., New Jersey (May 7, 1923)
Dear Doctor [Meigs],
    Would you kindly give me some advice on the following? I am 21 years old, and am a weak sickly girl; I am too nervous to go out to work for a living. So I am keeping company with a young man 23 years old. He said if I would marry him I would not need to go out to work. But how could I prevent from having children? I know I would never be able to carry a child or go through child birth in the condition I am in now. So would you be so kind and tell me how I can prevent from having them, as I think with rest and free[dom] from worry I may be able to have children in a few years, as I dearly love them and would like to have one or two. But if I ever had any now they would only suffer from weakness and I would be left a complete nervous wreck. So dear doctor please give me your kind advise. I have an envelope enclosed for your dear reply. I thank you ever so much in advance. Yours Very Truly.

Mrs. M.L., Louisiana (August 27, 1927)
    I am coming to you by letter for advice. I am pregnant and need your help. I have been pregnant three months and have been sick most of the time. I have sick stomache, head aches, and feel tired and without any

Courage at all. I do all my own housework and besides
have four little children to care for; the oldest one is only
seven years old. I would appreciate you telling me how to
control child birth. I have tried several ways but to no
good. I dont have any hard labor at birth. Very seldom
sick over an hour or two, but I have children so fast it is
wrecking my life. I am nervous at times.

Would like to receive advice from you and to receive
your monthly bulletins on how to care for myself through
the six months to follow. Will be glad to receive any
information that you can furnish on these subjects.

Mrs. H.H., Michigan (September 2, 1927)
Miss Margaret Sangers pamphlets.

Will you please send me one of your birth control? I
am married woman of 23 and have two children, and I
hope I wont have any more for a present time, becuase I
am having lots of trouble from my husban[d]. He wont
hard[l]y work. I am afraid I had to support my family so
help me please. I love children and all that, but in my
Condition two is enough for me to sup[p]ort. Yours truly.

Mrs. E.S., Kansas (January 13, 1928)
Dear Sirs:—

I have followed your book on Infant Care and found
it Wanderful. But I'm comming with my largest problem.
I am Mother of 2 little boys 1 yr apart & expect to be
mother again this summer. Im only in my twenties. We
Rent a farm & find it a hard row to hoe to provide food &
clothe for us all. We can not meet expenses. My health is

going down hill from hard Work & Bearing babies. My
husband works hard & worries, also has the Asthama so
bad in Winter I find My self doing a Man's Work. This is
hard to be Mother, Wife, & especially the out side Work.
   Now what I Want to know is Why can't We poor
people be given Birth Control as well as Dr's. & the Rich
people that could provide [for] & Dr. their families. We
need help to prevent any more babies. After this next one
comes Im going to seek advice if Possible so We can live
more happy. Don't you think it better to be Parents of 3
which we are willing to work & do all we can for them, to
raise & provide food for us all, then to hafto have 6 or
more that would take us down into the grave & leave 6 or
more for poverty to take & be Motherless? I think it
unfair Dr's. & Rich seek Birth Control & the poor can't
seek nothing, only Poverty & more babies. Any safe
Advice of where to go or do. Im willing to undergo
anything after our next baby comes to make me steral.
Birth Control, I b[e]lieve in it strong to keep down
divorce cases & Poverty, also so many a Criminal Case.
Please advice us. Thanking you in advance. Please don't
publish this letter with my name signed to it thou[gh] I'm
sure it would be enjoyed by the Poor class of people. I am
Resp.

Mrs. G.L., Michigan (August 20, 1929)
Dear Mrs. Abbott:—
   Or aren't you the person in charge now? Anyhow,
has our government any pamphlet on Birth Control? If so,
I'm sure we are eligible for a copy. We have been married
almost 10 years and have five little children. Our business:

hat cleaning and shoe shining. Our home almost paid for.
No car. No maid or other help. Sicknesses every year.
Bills! Wife very tired. She's 38. Husband, grey and 36.
Having to keep on child bearing strikes absolute terror to
wife's heart. Is there no acceptable safe preventative
measure husband would not complain about and not
painful to the mother? This is confidential—not for
reporters.

Perhaps it costs a dime or is sent free by Rep. Woodruff.
I have two good pamphlets on "Infant Care" and "Child
Care Pre-School." We have others on floors, leather,
heating, plants, goats, bird houses. If the government
can't help us now, we'll feel pretty badly. Would you like
to send me two on "Child Care" and "Infant Care" or at
least the latter for me to pass on to a new mother whose
first baby cries all the time? I'm not sure of her address or
would mail it. Thanking you. I am yours sincerely.

I Am Not Asking
for Charity

One result of the growing publicity accorded child welfare
was that poor women began to feel entitled to health care
and state aid. In the 1920s, rumors of government compensation for large families spread across the country, probably
as a result of confusion over the terms of the Sheppard-
Towner Act and the debate over maternity allowances in
European countries. Two of the dozens of letters the Children's Bureau received on this subject are included here.

Other women and their husbands wrote to the Bureau to inquire about the effects of the Sheppard-Towner Act, to ask it to intercede with other government agencies, or to ask for money for their families or communities.

Mrs. F.D., Arkansas (March 18, 1915)
To the United States Department of Labor:
    Please Send me the bulletins of Children's bureau. If uncle Sam Can do [us] any good We as farmers shure do need it, for we cant hardly get Bread for our babies. I am glad that you and miss Lathrop have care for our Children. I see your offer in the Country Gentelmen Paper. Ans. soon.

Mrs. F.B., Montana (July 19, 1919)
Dear Madam
    I received several pamp[h]lets from your Bureau of Child Welfare & placed them in the hands of young mothers whom I think will derive great benefit therefrom. I am at your service to distribute any number of them. My letter to you now is to seek your support & help to get Gov. aid for the Farmers wifes & children of this district. This part of montana has been stricken for a third year with drought, so completely that many of the little children must suffer from scarcity of food & clothing. I understand the Judge of this county & several gentelman who know the terrible conditions here have taken the matter up with Red Cross officials, soliciting tempor[ar]y help until the Gov. could give relief, but without avail, & I beg of you to do every thing possible to help these

mothers to feed & clothe these children in their homes. Some of the familys are living entirely on what the cows are producing & just as soon as cold weather sets in & the cows dry up, [they] will be not only without food for the stock, but without means to provide common necessities for these children.

When the war came we of the farms sent our boys to fight for flag & country. Thoes boys were phisically mentally & morally fit to march endure or fight. 20 years from now, who knows, we may need another army, and if this Gov. will cool[l]y sit & shut their ears to the crys of our children for food what sort of men do they expect to call to arms? It is all very well to feed Germany but charity begins at home, & it is up to our officials at Washington whether these children shall grow up & say "Our Gov let us starve whilst they fed the Huns" & therefore be ashamed of their citizenship, or bless the day that gave them birth on American soil.

I know the nearest thing to your heart is the welfare of Montana's children; as your special Bulletin No. 4 states, Our children are the nation's Wealth. Shall we not feed them first of all? I hope you will take this letter direct to his [Excellency] president wilson & tell him [that] without Gov. aid, Montana is in worse condition than any country in Europe. When he called upon we farmers to sow every possible acre to wheat, they responded & mor[t]gaged everything possible in order to sow thoes extra acres. These Banks have gone beyond the principles of good banking in order to help us, now it is all gone, & unless we get financial aid at once to feed our stock & take care of these children, America will never be able to look the next generation squar[e]ly in the face. Trusting you will give us your aid & answers soon. I remain yours respectfully, A Farmer Wife.

Lathrop responds that although she read Mrs. F.B.'s letter with "deep sympathy and I trust with some understanding," the Children's Bureau has no funds for the sort of work needed in Montana. She refers Mrs. F.B.'s letter to the Red Cross, "which I trust may lead to some substantial aid."

Mrs. M.M., California (July 29, 1920)
Dear Sir.

I was just reading your little booklet on "What do growing children need." And it says at the end, "Is your child getting a squar[e] deal? If not, what are you going to do about it?" Well, this is what I am going to do about it. I am going to state the condition of things.

I am the mother of seven little tots. The oldest one only 8 years and the last two are twins. We lost our twin girl last Dec. 8, which leaves 6 little mouths to feed & 6 little bodies to keep clean & clothed. They are kept clean and are well clothed but they do not get what they ought to have to eat. They never see a glass of milk. Certified milk is 23 cents a quart here and other milk 15 cents a quart. They never have meat and very seldom have eggs as they are 50 cents a doz. here. My husband only makes $4 a day, and he never worked a stroke last winter as he had a broken foot.

Now there ought not to be such a thing as 6 dear little kiddies not having the propper food to eat. There are a great many men & women working for the Children Welfare Bureau. If each one could put in a dime they could get those little tots a good jersey cow and we would

not sell only milk enough to buy feed when there is no
green feed. I could make butter which they never have
because it is .75 lb. I am not begging & neither am I
doing this for myself but am simply answering the question
asked in your booklet: & for my babies. You know a man
cant feed 6 children properly on $4 a day, pay rent, water,
and clothe them, besides there is his wife & himself to
feed & clothe. Respectfully.

Mrs. J.S., Colorado (received June 6, 1921)
     If I were a painter I should paint a picture of a farm
mother and three babies. The babies aged four weeks,
2 years and four years. I should paint her picture in her
kitchen with a view of the clothes-line of clothing, her
morning's work, to be seen through the open door-way;
and the child of four, whom the distracted mother does
not observe, coming in at the door with muddy feet.
Washing is an almost every day's task where there are
three babies, so the wash would certainly belong in the
picture. Through the window I would picture three other
representatives of her work: the cow, the chickens and a
garden. But the rotten garden fence would be breaking to
let in the cow, and chickens and a sow and pigs to eat
up her hard labors in the garden, and the sow would be
eating the chickens. And this too would be *very* true to
life, for the average country woman must see her hard
labors in poultry-raising be destroyed by hogs as well as
hawks, crows and varmints.
     In the room I should picture the mother trying to pacify
the crying young baby by carrying it as she sets dinner
on the table for some husky men. The two year old would

be upsetting a bucket of slop or pan of wash-water, or digging the ashes from the hearth; for those stunts are typical of two-year-olds whose mothers are too distracted to observe their doings. There would be a basket of vegetables and some buckets of fruit and some fruit jars to show the mother's afternoon's work, for she has to can fruit on wash day or not at all. I'd picture the men eating glut[t]onously, while the husband, overworked in his efforts to farm a half improved farm and raise the money to pay rent to satisfy the greedy owner—who demands as much rent as if the farm were well improved—the husband would be saying, "The man et works hes t' eat!" And I'd picture the landowner who has come to collect his rent—and who has been advising the young man before they came to dinner on how he can manage to have the rent money—whisper[ing] advise against "raisin' brats." I'd picture him eating, while he says for the young wife's benefit, "Its a woman's place t' mek the livin' 'n help a man git ahead 'n hev somethin'!"

And over this picture I'd picture the shadows of three women looking on, not present in reality; but present in their thoughts, because they know what the young mother is suffering. And one, the wife of the landowner, would be saying, "She's a fool to be rais[ing] them brats; if I'd raised a family for my man to provide for he'd never a been able to own this farm!" And one, the mother of the young man, would be saying, "I raised *my two*! And she can raise her'n! If I'd go and help her with her work 'n mek things easy for her, she wouldn't care how many brats she has for my boy to provide for. She'd just keep his nose t' the grindstone 'n he'd never hev nothin'!"

And the other womanshadow, the sister of the young

mother would be saying, "I helped take care of the other one 'n I told her then I'd not to help take care of another one. If she has another one 'n works like this, she'll break down; I've told her so, too, 'n I've told her nobody wants t' take care of her kids for her!" And I'd picture the mother's face with dawning hardness and bitterness and intense suffering written accross it. And the title of the picture would be, "How long will our young mothers endure?"

I paid little heed to the advice and commands of others against my children's lives: I heeded the criticisms of statesmen and preachers against mothers who do not raise their children. One National Congressman said, "The country is the best place for children, there should be more children in the country." I have five young children and have had to help make the living for them: now I am so broken down I can scarcely do for them. My doctor says I need an operation and a year's rest to rebuild my health. But we have no money for an operation, much less to hire help with my work until I can regain my strength. Though we run a 20 cow dairy and raise lots of grain and feed, and my husband is known as the best worker and most efficient farmer around; yet so low are our finances that we cannot pay the premium on his $1,000 life insurance due in June. We do not see how we are to raise the money to pay the interest on the mortgage on our cows due in Sept., for it takes all we can make from the dairy to pay the rent and ranch expenses. We cannot even hire help, but must depend on our little girls aged 10 and 13 to help in dairy and field and haying and harvesting. Ever since I can remember there has been a campaign of education of mothers and children on how they can make the living in the country. Isn't it about time to have a campaign of

education of our country *men* on how *they* can make the
living for their wives and children instead of being merely
able to provide for the cattle?

Aren't there American Organizations that can help
American young fathers and mothers to have homes of
their own for their children in the country, instead of
living in shacks here, there, or yonder on someone else's
land? Isn't there one Organization in America to see to it
that *American* country mothers and children have medical
attention? Some way to make it possible for our American
young men to make a living over and above paying the
rent or buying homes? Yours very Respectfully.

P.S. We can[n]ot have vegetables or poultry because it
takes all of our work to run the ranch to pay the rent. If
we rent a smaller ranch, there are no buildings to protect
our stock; much less a house fit for a family to live in. And
the rent charged for small, poorly improved ranches, is
even higher per acre than for the large, well improved
ranches.

Mrs. J.S. (July 10, 1921)

I want to thank you for your literature on Home
Economics. I have studied it for possible ideas, but we
haven't the wherewithal to come up to even those plain
meals. I feed my family at a cost of about three cents per
1000 calories. This difference is partly due to having to
do without some kinds of food and partly due to difference
in food cost. As for instance milk in your pamp[h]let is
priced at 13 c per qt. We don't receive that amount per
gal. We sell sweet, pure cream testing 20 per cent butter
fat, and receive only 6 cts per qt or 3 cts. per lb. . . .

We don't have fresh fruit and vegetables. We can't pay

the price asked at the store and we can't raise them. In the first place, though this ranch is rented as a well-improved ranch, there is no means for irrigation for fruit and vegetables. Second, no plot fenced off from hogs and chickens. Third, we're all so overworked trying to take the place of hired hands, because we don't make enough to pay even a dollar a day for hired help, that we have little strength and time left for gardening. Though we're trying to have a garden at back side of ranch 1/2 mi away, and tend it with team.

Next year we hope to be able to buy fencing for nearby garden spot. But unless we can rent the place for a period of 5 yrs we can not afford to install an irrigation system, as we have no water for such purpose except by some costly means. And to go to such expens[e] would only mean the ranch would be more likely to be sold and we'd have to move. We have seen more than one such case. Where renter would work to build up the soil and go to the expense of repairing buildings and fences, only to have the rent raised or the place be sold because of his labors and expense.

Can't the Children's Bureau plead for a law allowing or compel[l]ing a five year lease, so that the renters can have an opportunity to be more than tramps or campers? They are criticised for not doing better by the farms; but they are the victims of the one year lease. The land owners won't lease except for a year at a time, because they want to be free to sell at a high price when the opportunity offers. Most of the young children of the country districts are in the homes of renters and hired hands; and our laws are all in favor of the land owners and large stock raisers. The land is not priced according to what men can pay and provide for their families, but the price is set by batchelors, and by men who have no children, or whose families are small or nearly grown. Such men, and men who already own land, can pay a higher price for land than young fathers can: If the national gov't can pass laws to protect stock, can make restrictions to eliminate cattle ticks and cattle diseases, and so forth: why can't the national gov't make rulings for the protection of young children in the country? Why can't the national gov't make rulings with regard to leases; kind of houses for renters and hired hands; and handy, abundant sanitary water supplies; sewage systems; and the price of land?

Why not put a heavy tax on the big land owners unless they conform to humanitarian laws for the benefit of the children of hired hands and renters?

Mrs. L.W., Alabama (March 13, 1922)

Please send me Miscellaneous Series No. 6. I read Senator Caper Washington Letter in Hous[e]hold some time back that Congress had passed the Maternity Bill; if so I sure am glad.

I do hope it will help us Poor Country people who need help. We live on a farm and have very hard work to do. I am 27 yrs. old and have Five Little one's to Care for besides my husband an[d] his Father.

Mrs. L.G., Pennsylvania (April 11, 1922):

Dear Miss Abbott:-

Your kind letter of March 3 was received and I have read very carefully all of the printed matter send with

same. Now to explain my reason for inquiry. I am a
member of our little Parent-Teacher Assn. here, and one
of the other members came to me one day and told me
that a bill had been passed which would compell all
women who were one month pregnant to go to the Court
House and register, that the government would then
appoint a physician to look after you and the child when
born, and then the government could come into your
home at any time and remove the child, claiming it as the
property of the government. Of course this didn't appeal
to me and when one mother got up in the next meeting
and asked that a petition be circulated and signed to down
the bill in this State I was named on the Committee to
procure signers against it. Well, rather than take
newspaper talk as a foundation for my petition I wrote at
once to our Congressman, Mr. Edgar R. Kiess, for a copy
of the Maternity Bill which he promptly sent me, and as I
could see not[h]ing to object to I then wrote you, and the
more I read of it the more sure I feel that it is wonderful
. . . .

I am a Mother of five children, the oldest a girl of eight
years and the youngest are twins just two years old, girls.
We are people of very moderate means and when our
twins were born the attending physician's bill was $50.00
which was $25.00 more than we could afford. Then when
the babies were six weeks old they were losing so steadily
that I was greatly alarmed and called in a baby specialist
who came twice a week for 15 weeks just to give me
instructions on how to feed the babies so they would
thrive. I paid him $2.00 each time he came and I never
begrudged it tho I had to do without many things I wanted
and needed so as to pay the Doctor.

One of my neighbors across the street from me here lost

her baby when nearly three months old, because she couldn't afford to have the Dr, as I had done.

I wish that the women who buy such magazines as "The Ladies Home Journal" and "Good Housekeeping" and others would read the wonderful articles on this subject which are printed in those books. I think that it is through ignorance of what they talk about that causes so many women to blunder into getting up these petitions. Can you give me a true list of the names of the women who thought out this Bill, and how many are *unmarried?* Respectfully.

Abbott writes that she is "very much interested" in Mrs. L. G.'s experience and that of her neighbor, and tells her that "it was largely out of many, many letters of exactly this sort and our own experience in the field that the plan for the Sheppard-Towner Maternity Act was formulated." She credits Lathrop with the drawing of the bill but stresses that there was consultation with doctors, social workers, and mothers, and that the bill had the support of the National Congress of Mothers and Parent-Teacher Associations and the Women's Joint Legislative Committee. "It was demanded by literally millions of mothers in the country." She says that most Sheppard-Towner work will be done by unmarried women, nurses, and doctors who are especially trained in the field and who would, "except in rare instances, not be able to do the work if they had children of their own." She tells Mrs. L. G. that the author of the first Children's Bureau bulletins was a mother and that the reports on milk and other factors were done by a doctor who was also a mother. "They were, however, not selected because they were mothers but because, in addition to being mothers, they had the technical information which made what they had to say of real value to mothers who were looking for expert advice."

Mrs. T.L., Illinois (July 21, 1922)
Dear Sirs:—

On the 24th March 1922 Triplets were born [to] Mrs.
T.L., all girls weighing at birth, G. five lb. C. 4 1/2 lb. and
D. 4 1/2 lb. And I would like the Gover[n]ment to help
me out with them for I got another one besides them, a
little boy two years old. And my husband dont make very
much mon[e]y and we got to pay rent. They weigh now
G. 7 1/2 lb, C. 7-15-4 and D. 7-1-6.

Please help me out to raise them.

Mr. W.C., St. Louis, Missouri (October 18, 1924)
Dear Sir or Madam

I have a daughter born on Oct. 15 1922, so that
makes her just 2 years and 3 days old. And from the
information which my wife rec'd from the different
booklets (either one or two of them) issued by the U.S.
Dept. of Labor, Wash. D.C., she has been able to raise
her to be a baby that anyone would and should be proud
of. And I must say that her Daddy is proud of her. She
weighs just around or between 31 and 33 lbs. and I am
enclosing her picture for the Children's Bureau to look at
and also to show proof of what I say.

This is our first child and my wife did not know the
first thing about children, for her mother always kept
her ignorant of such things. Even after the child was born,
she did not tell her a thing, and it was only due to the
first class information which was given her through your
good books that she was able to raise the child to be what
she is.

But there is one difficulty which she is now having

trouble to overcome, and that is the child is never a
hungary baby. In the morning she spends about one hour
to feed the baby a bowl of Scotch oats and later on some
orange juice and some kind of fruit and also some milk.
(She is given one quart of Pevely Milk each day and the
only way she will take it gladly is in the Bottle but we
are of the opinion that she is too big to take the Bottle.)
(A suggestion from your Bureau will help us.) And then
during the day she is given a dish of vegetables such as
carrots, string beans, etc. She will not eat bread, but
rather likes Butter, always eats the Butter off the Bread.

And in regards to her Bath, why her mother gives her a
bath such as the average Baby *does not get*. She places the
Baby on the table which is all prepared and then starts by
cleaning out the nostrils with a toothpick covered with
cotton. And then she has an eyedropper with which she
drops a solution into her eyes of Boric Acid. And then she
washes her body, and after that is done, she places her in
the large Bath tub which is partly filled with warm water.
And then she finishes the job by pouring cold water on
her. In all, it takes just a little over one hour.

Now in regards to myself. I am a disabled soldier,
having been awarded Vocational Training with pay under
Section 2. For 2 years I was with the RR here in St. Louis
and, although I did complain to the Veterans bureau that
I was not learning a thing which would in any way help
me, still they kept me there. And when my time (2 years)
was up, the Gov't was paying me $145.00 per month so
they made arrangements with the RR, where by I was
given a job for 100.00 per month, which I took, thinking
that I would be awarded a few dollars each month as
compensation from the Gov't. But instead of that, I was

turned down on my claim, due as they say my illness could
not be traced to Army service, even though I was awarded
Vocational Training—something which I would not
accept if I thought for a minute that I did not have it
coming to me. Prior to Army service, I was making
around or between $150.00 to $200.00 per month, so you
can imagine how I was to get along on 100.00 per month
and pay all my expenses! It was only through a good friend
of the U.S. Soldier that I was able to obtain a position
with [another] RR at a salary of 135.00 per month, which
is really just about keeping Bread and Butter on the table.
And I can assure you that we are not having any good
times, for we cannot really go to see a show unless we
deprive the Baby of something, and that is just what I will
not do. I only wish that through someone I would be able
to get my case to General Hines. I know that he is a very
Broad Minded person and does not know or realize that
any soldier is receiving this kind of treatment. If it be
possible that through your good office my case be given a
rehearing, I will assure you that you will be helping the
Baby daughter and my Wife as well as my self, and it will
be highly appreciated.

I am writing to you from the RR office, as I want to try
and do something in regards to my case and then surprise
my wife. Trusting that you will be able to help me.
Respectfully.

*Hull writes that "it is very pleasant for us to be given a
share in the upbringing of this little girl." She advises that the
child should have been weaned from the bottle before two years
of age and should be getting away from "infantile habits." She
also suggests that she is a little heavy and probably overfed. She
adds that if the child does not eat the proper amount of food, the*

*parents should put it away and offer it again at the next meal.
She also advises Mr. W.C. that the bath is too long and the use
of boric acid can lower the natural resistance of the child's
tissues. She sends a copy of Mr. W.C.'s letter to the Veterans'
Bureau.*

Mrs. E. R., Idaho (July 6, 1928)
Dear Sir.,

I wish to know if the government gives any reward to
mother's of triplets. I gave birth to triplets May 31st and
have five other children. Some tell me that the
gover[n]ment makes the mother a gift. I am not asking for
charity but if it is customary to do so I would surely like to
have it. I cannot even afford to buy a buggy for the babies,
so I could make use of the reward.

I hope I'm not doing any harm in asking this and don't
expect any charity unless the government does reward
mothers in this way. If it does I feel I'm entitled to my
reward. Will you please answer this anyway? Res'p.

Mrs. C.E., Alabama (April 1, 1931)
Dear Sirs

I am sending you a picture of my three (3) sets of
twins. I am a mother of thirteen children, three sets of
twins. I think I ought to have a prize for that hardly ever
happen. All of them is living. If you think I ought to have
a prize I will thank you all so much. Please send my
picture back. And if you dought my word I will refure you
to the following names. I will apperciate what you do.
Your truly.

Appendix

The original Children's Bureau correspondence is located among the Children's Bureau Records (Record Group 102, Central Files, 1914–1940) at the National Archives in Washington, D.C. In keeping with the filing system of the agency, the letters have been arranged chronologically by subject. Subject files are collected in groups dated 1914–1920, 1921–1924, 1925–1928, and 1929–1932. Although the letters contained in this book are drawn primarily from the subject files on maternal and infant health care (4-3, 4-4, and 4-5), I have also included letters from the subject files on the Sheppard-Towner Act (10-12) and mothers' pensions (9-4).

To facilitate the reader's access to the original documents, this appendix lists the date and file number of each letter (arranged in the order in which it appears in the book). In order to retrieve the original letter from Mrs. G.W. of Iowa (dated March 30, 1916), the reader would simply request file 4-3-1-4-3 from the chronological group 1914–1920.

Chapter 1. Before the Baby Comes
Now I Am Pregnant, and I Get So Nervous and Worry So Terrible
    Mrs. G.W., Iowa, March 30, 1916   4-3-1-4-3
    Mrs. A.P., Wyoming, October 19, 1916   4-3-0-3

Mrs. E.G., Indiana, June 18, 1918   4-2-1-5
Mrs. H.R., Georgia, June 14, 1920   4-2-0-3
Mrs. C.T., Tennessee, June 29, 1921   4-4-2-2
Mrs. M.A., Minnesota, October 19, 1921   4-4-3-3
Mrs. W.M., Wisconsin, November 28, 1924   4-4-2-3
Mrs. B.S., New York, September 28, 1926   4-4-2-2
Mrs. H.H., West Virginia, October 17, 1927   4-4-2-2
Mrs. J.P., Ohio, November 17, 1927   4-4-2-2
I Would Far Rather Ask You Than Mother
Mrs. G.W., Missouri, May 29, 1918   4-4-3-3
Mrs. G.B., Oregon, February 9, 1921   4-4-0
Mrs. W.O., Illinois, August 17, 1921   4-4-1-0
Mrs. D.O., New Mexico, December 19, 1921   4-4-1-2
Miss M.K., Illinois, February 22, 1922   4-4-1-1
Mrs. F.S., Ohio, July 31, 1922   4-4-3-6
Mrs. E.M., Indiana, January 22, 1925   4-4-1-1
Mrs. R.L., Idaho, November 5, 1926   4-4-2-2
Mrs. E.B., Mississippi, August 18, 1927   4-4-1
Mrs. O.B., Missouri, February 23, 1932   4-6-0

Chapter 2. Raising the Baby
*There Is Too Much Foolishness Attached to
the Feeding of Children*
Mrs. N.W., Texas, February 2, 1916   4-3-1-4-3
Mrs. R.L., New York, May 10, 1919   4-4-3-2
Mrs. E.I., Iowa, March 24, 1920   4-4-3-3
Successful Farming, December 29, 1920   4-5-3
   (in 1921–1924 files)
Mrs. L.R., Montana, November 4, 1923   4-5-3-0
Mrs. C.A., Michigan, March 2, 1926   4-4-4-2
Mrs. N.B., Michigan, July 20, 1926   4-5-3-1
Mrs. J.B., South Dakota, March 4, 1927   4-5-3-1

Mrs. C.S., New Jersey, April 6, 1927   4-5-3-2

Miss G.M., Pennsylvania, March 22, 1928   4-5-3-2

I Shall Be Glad to Learn How to Cure This Habit

Mrs. F.H., Nebraska, July 5, 1915   4-4

Mrs. J.S., Washington, D.C., January 10,
    1920   4-4-3-1-2

Mrs. W.P., Ohio, January 26, 1922   4-5-7-2

Mrs. R.C., New Jersey, April 4, 1923   4-5-7-2-3

Mrs. O.G., California, December 19, 1923   4-6-0

Mrs. N.F., New Mexico, February 28, 1924   4-5-7-2-1

Mrs. J.L., Illinois, November 7, 1925   4-6-7-2-1

Mrs. D.F., New Jersey, May 11, 1927   4-5-7-2-3

Mrs. W.G., Texas, August 27, 1927   4-5-5

Mrs. J.T., Wisconsin, September 8, 1927   4-5-7-2-5
    (in 1921–1924 files)

A Dirty Child at Three Months Is a Mother's Disgrace

Mrs. E.R., California, May 16, 1918   4-4-7-4

Mrs. R.B., Pennsylvania, November 9, 1924   4-5-6-4

Mrs. F.S., Massachusetts, December 12, 1925   4-5-6-4

Mrs. L.S., Ohio, January 30, 1928   4-5-6-4

I Worry Myself Nearly to Death with Him

Mrs. E.C., Kentucky, September 23, 1915   4-4-3-1-3

Mrs. N.W., Texas, February 18, 1916   4-3-1-4-3

Mrs. H.S., Virginia, December 4, 1917   4-5-3-1-3

Mrs. O.W., Washington, March 17, 1918   4-4-3-1

Mrs. G.W., Maryland, April 15, 1918   4-4-3-2

Mrs. W.D., Pennsylvania, April 17, 1918   4-4-3-2

Mrs. F.D., Quebec, December 18, 1921   4-5-8-1

Mrs. L.L., Maine, May 23, 1922   4-5-6-2

Mrs. W.F., Missouri, August 1, 1925   4-5-8-1

They Brought Him to the Door in His Little Casket

Mrs. L.W., Iowa, January 17, 1916   4-3-2-4

Mrs. W.D., New York, September 10, 1917   4-4-0

Mrs. W.D., Massachusetts, June 22, 1918   4-4-0-3
Mrs. F.W., Michigan, June 25, 1918   8-6-2-2-3
Mrs. C.A., Missouri, November 11, 1924   4-4-3-5
Mrs. S.L., Louisiana, August 12, 1926   4-4-3-4
Mrs. G.B., Missouri, February 11, 1932   4-5-18

Chapter 3. Motherhood: All Work and No Money

I Am Busy All Day But My Work Is Never Done
Mrs. M.T., Texas, June 23, 1916   4-6-0-3
Mrs. N.W., Washington, March 4, 1920   4-10-5
Mrs. H.P., Kansas, July 28, 1921   4-10-6-0
There Is No Way of Buying the Most Needy Things
Mrs. M.R., Idaho, January 4, 1916   4-3-0-3
Mrs. W.S., New York, January 30, 1918   9-4-4-1
Mrs. A.G., Kansas, August 10, 1921   4-10-6-0
Mrs. S.D., California, September 7, 1921   4-10-6-1
Mrs. A.F., Arkansas, July 15, 1927   4-4-2-2
Mrs. D.B., Pennsylvania, May 19, 1932   4-6-2-2
My Heart Aches for the Poor Children
Miss A.R., New Jersey, March 7, 1915   4-5-0-3
Mrs. H.S., Mississippi, July 7, 1916   4-5-0
Mrs. W.J., California, June 6, 1917   4-4-3-1
Mrs. E.M., Missouri, June 22, 1917   4-4-0-3
Our Government Ought to Protect Us
Mrs. H.B., Illinois, February 28, 1916   4-2-0-3
Mrs. G.H., North Carolina, October 5, 1917   9-4-4-1
Mrs. W.P., California, May 20, 1918   9-4-4-1
Mrs. G.A., Pennsylvania, April 13,
    1927   10-12-2-5(40)
Mrs. J.S., Illinois, May 9, 1927   10-12-2-5(15)

Mrs. S.W., Florida, May 19, 1927   4-10-6-1

Mrs. M.S., Minnesota, August 20,
   1927   10-12-2-5(25)

I Suffered Hell on Earth because of a Doctor

Mrs. W.M., Virginia, March 29, 1915   4-5-0-3

Mrs. H.A., Wyoming, July 2, 1918   4-4-0-3

Mrs. A.T., Missouri, March 28, 1922   4-4

Mrs. R.P., Iowa, February 19, 1924   4-4-2-2

Mrs. W.I., Michigan, April 15, 1924   4-4-2-2

Mrs. M.M., Indiana, March 3, 1926   4-5-6-3

Mrs. P.O., Iowa, July 23, 1928   4-5-6-3

Mrs. E.H., Michigan, January 9, 1931   4-6-0

Mrs. R.C., Florida, January 27, 1932   4-5-7-3-1

Mrs. A.E., Minnesota, August 10, 1932   4-5-7

I Have Children So Fast It Is Wrecking My Life

Mrs. T.M., North Dakota, October 14, 1921   4-4-1-3

Miss L.A., New Jersey, May 7, 1923   4-4-1-3

Mrs. M.L., Louisiana, August 27, 1927   4-4-1-3

Mrs. H.H., Michigan, September 2, 1927   4-4-1-3

Mrs. E.S., Kansas, January 13, 1928   4-4-1-3

Mrs. G.L., Michigan, August 20, 1929   4-4-4-1

I Am Not Asking for Charity

Mrs. F.D., Arkansas, March 18, 1915   4-5-0-3

Mrs. F.B., Montana, July 19, 1919   4-4-0-3

Mrs. M.M., California, July 29, 1920   4-6-0-3

Mrs. J.S., Colorado, June 6, 1921   4-10-6-1

Mrs. L.W., Alabama, March 13, 1922   11-2-2

Mrs. L.G., Pennsylvania, April 11, 1922   11-40-2

Mrs. T.L., Illinois, July 21, 1922   4-4-1-4

Mr. W.C., Missouri, October 18, 1924   4-5-3-0

Mrs. E.R., Idaho, July 6, 1928   4-4-1-4

Mrs. C.E., Alabama, April 1, 1931   4-5-7-3-4

Index

Abbott, Grace: career of, 8, 10–11, 23; and social security, 31–32; correspondence, 58, 140, 195; and birth control, 180
Abortion, 61, 62–63, 65–66, 178
Addams, Jane, 9
Aid to Dependent Children, 5, 32
American Medical Association, 25
Anderson, Viola Russell: correspondence, 58, 59, 60, 67, 78, 79, 81, 82, 83, 92, 93, 97, 141, 168

Baker, S. Josephine, 26, 47
Birth control: 9, 14, 26, 179; inquiries, 52, 68, 174, 180–184
Birth registration, 18, 20, 37, 162
Bottlefeeding: 16–17, 59, 73, 80; artificial formula, 48, 82, 83, 107
Breastfeeding: 16–17, 20, 107; technique, 38, 78, 81; difficulties of insufficient milk supply, 59–60, 78, 79, 80–81, 118–119; difficulties of overfeeding, 104, 117; difficulties of mother's inadequate diet, 148–149

Charity, 148, 149–150, 186
Child Health Association, 25
Child labor, 5, 8, 10, 18
Child welfare: 118–119, 141, 144, 145; baby week, 20, 118, 145; Children's Year, 20–21; conference on standards, 21
Childbirth: 2, 13, 138, 171–172; death in, 11, 14, 47; medical intervention in, 11, 14, 16, 123–125, 162; dread of, 14, 16, 49, 150, 184; injuries from, 14, 49, 102, 162, 163, 173–174, 176–178; time in labor, 48, 80, 116–117, 171, 173–174, 182; without medical or nursing care, 49, 55, 139; signs of labor, 68; use of instruments, 123–125, 173–174
Children: as national asset, 55, 186
Children's Bureau: correspondence, 2–4, 5; role in establishment of welfare programs, 5, 46; establishment of, 6–7; staff, 8–12; and mothers, 12, 45–46; early history, 17–21, 133, 135; investigations of infant mortality, 18; investigations of infant mortality in Johnstown, Pennsylvania,

207